Dumplings for Beginners

DUMPLINGS
for beginners

50 Recipes and Simple Step-by-Step Lessons to Make Your Favorite Dumplings

TERRI DIEN

callisto publishing
an imprint of Sourcebooks

Copyright © 2021 by Callisto Publishing LLC

Cover and internal design © 2021 by Callisto Publishing LLC

Cover Photography: ©Aubrie Legault/Stocksy

Illustrations: © 2021 Ohn Mar Win

Interior Photography: p. ii: Hung Quach/Stocksy; p. v: @Jan-Peter Westermann/Stockfood; pp. vi-vii: ©Shaiith/Shutterstock; p. ix: ©Marc Tran/Stocksy; p. x: ©Enjoy The Life/Shutterstock; p. 16: ©Giada Canu/Stocksy; p. 34: ©Dorling Kindersley ltd / Alamy Stock Photo; p. 48: ©AS Food Studio/Shutterstock; p. 68: ©Ina Peters/Stocksy; p. 88: ©from my point of view/Shutterstock

Author photograph by Carolyn Shek

Cover recipe: Shu Mai, page 50

Interior and Cover Designer: Jami Spittler

Art Producer: Janice Ackerman

Editor: Annie Choi

Production Editor: Matthew Burnett

Production Manager: Riley Hoffman

Published by Callisto Publishing LLC C/O Sourcebooks LLC
P.O. Box 4410, Naperville, Illinois 60567-4410
(630) 961-3900
callistopublishing.com

Printed and bound in China.
OGP 19

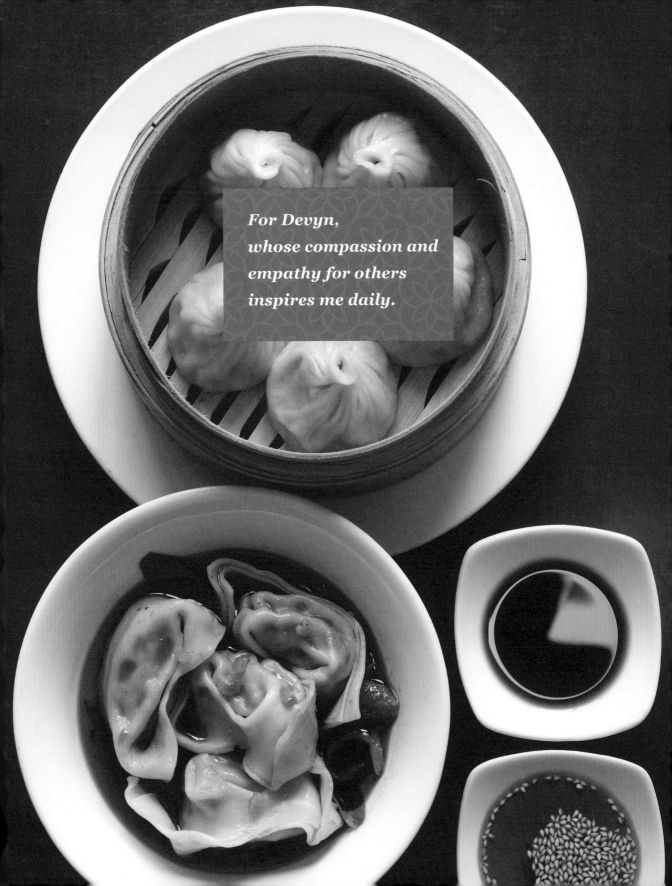

*For Devyn,
whose compassion and
empathy for others
inspires me daily.*

Contents

INTRODUCTION

Dumplings are little parcels of love—juicy presents on a plate bringing happiness with every bite. I've been making and eating dumplings all my life. As a child, it was a way to spend quality time with my mom. She taught me how to salt cabbage and make pickled radishes, and together we folded dozens of wontons she would freeze and cook later.

Dumplings also helped stretch the family food budget. A filling made with ground pork and vegetables stuffed into small wrappers could feed our family of four comfortably with a little over a half pound of meat per batch. Just four dumplings could fill me up for lunch, but of course, I always ate way more! But we didn't just make these at home—we also went out for dim sum and devoured stacks of steamer baskets filled with shu mai and har gow, arguing over who should get the last char siu bao.

Right after culinary school, I taught cooking classes. My first-ever dumpling class was for a couple who flew from Minnesota to the Bay Area just to learn how to make wrappers and fillings from scratch. I spent weeks developing authentic recipes for them, simplifying the process for beginners. Since then, I've taught hundreds of dumpling classes, and during every class, I pause for a moment to

observe my students at work—a relaxed group folding dumplings and chatting happily with one another.

For me, getting everyone involved is the best part about making dumplings at home. By bringing together friends and family to make dumplings, we get a chance to catch up and share funny stories. At the end of the process, we sit down and enjoy the fruits of our labor, savoring the delicious morsels we've created together.

This book includes 50 recipes and step-by-step instructions for making some of the most popular Asian dumplings and dim sum classics from scratch, such as shu mai, har gow, potstickers, and baos, plus various dipping sauces to serve with your favorite dumplings. You'll learn how to make your own wrappers and fillings and how to fold classic dumpling shapes as well as how to boil, steam, and pan-fry your dumplings. Where store-bought wrappers can come in handy, we won't be shy about using them. I'll also give you an overview of pantry staples and must-have tools necessary for dumpling success.

Remember, making dumplings at home is not just about making them from scratch; it's also about the communal experience. As the saying goes, "many hands make light work." Gather your loved ones around the table to make the dumplings with you. I promise the dumplings will taste so much better when everyone pitches in to help!

Shu Mai, page 50

1

DUMPLINGS MADE SIMPLE

This chapter introduces the ingredients, tools, and know-how you need to start your dumpling journey. Even if you've only ever had dumplings through takeout or at dim sum restaurants, you're in safe hands here. I'll guide you through everything you need to know to make dumplings from scratch at home.

Why Make Dumplings at Home?

There are many benefits to making dumplings at home. Perhaps you want to control what goes into your dumplings, or maybe you don't live near an Asian market to buy premade wrappers. For example, a friend has a shellfish allergy, which prevents her from going out for dim sum. Or, if you follow a gluten-free diet, you might have a hard time ordering safely in a restaurant. Whatever your motivation, this book will show you how to create authentic flavors with your own wrappers and fillings. Making dumplings is not exactly an easy process, but I'll break it down for you into doable steps.

What's in a Dumpling?

Most Asian dumplings consist of a piece of dough wrapped around a filling. There are many variations of dumpling wrappers and fillings as well as cooking methods. Dumplings can be bite-size or large, savory or sweet—but the most important qualities of a dumpling are the texture and flavor of its wrapper and filling. Wrappers can be crunchy, soft, chewy, or tender. Fillings must be extremely flavorful and tender. The possibility of combinations is endless!

This book covers some of the most well-loved traditional Asian dumplings that are boiled, steamed, pan-fried, or deep-fried. You'll get recipes for shu mai, har gow, fried wontons, and many other classics. The book also includes some steamed baos, which aren't technically dumplings but still encase a flavorful filling and are steamed and pan-fried just like dumplings.

The first dumplings are said to have originated more than 1,800 years ago in China during the Han dynasty. As the legend goes, one very cold winter, a man named Zhang Zhongjing returned to his village after traveling and found people starving. To help them, he cooked some meat, flavored it with herbs and spices, and wrapped small portions of the meat with scraps of dough. He folded the dumplings in a shape to resemble ears. He boiled the dumplings and served them to his community. The villagers were so grateful for his creation that they continued to make dumplings throughout the year in his honor.

Today, dumplings are enjoyed around the world. Nearly every cuisine features a dumpling-like dish that represents its own culture and flavors. And specifically, almost every Asian culture features dumplings that are similar in shape and cooking method with varying fillings and wrappers. Japanese gyozas, for example, are like Chinese potstickers: both are shaped into a pleated crescent and pan-fried.

ASIAN DUMPLING CHEAT SHEET

Bao: A fluffy steamed bun made from soft, yeasted dough; can be filled with savory or sweet fillings or enjoyed without filling.

Char siu bao: A steamed bun with a Chinese barbecue pork filling; technically not a dumpling but enjoyed with dim sum.

Gyoza: The Japanese potsticker; the filling can be similar to Chinese potstickers, but the wrapper is thinner, like a wonton wrapper.

Har gow: Steamed shrimp dumpling made with see-through crystal dumpling dough so the cooked shrimp inside shows through.

Jiaozi: Chinese steamed dumplings, usually enjoyed during Lunar New Year celebrations; often filled with ground pork and vegetables.

Mandu: Korean dumplings, generally folded using the wonton fold (with round wrappers) or pleated crescent fold; can be steamed, boiled, added to soup, or pan-fried.

Momo: Steamed dumplings filled with spiced ground meats and vegetables; these dumplings are enjoyed in the Tibet region of China, Nepal, Bhutan, and India.

Potsticker: Its Chinese name, *guotie*, translates to "wok stuck." It's a delicious accident—a cook let dumplings steam too long in the wok, resulting in nearly burnt bottoms that were crispy yet steamed.

Shengjian bao: This Shanghainese breakfast staple is a bao filled with savory fillings and pan-fried for a crispy bottom.

Shiu jiao: Its literal translation, "water dumpling," is the basic Chinese boiled dumpling. When steamed, this dumpling becomes a jiaozi. When pan-fried, it's a potsticker.

Shu mai: A popular steamed dumpling in dim sum restaurants, shu mai is small, cup-shaped, and typically filled with pork and shrimp.

Wonton: Named for its tortellini-like shape, wontons use thin, translucent wrappers made from flour and water; served boiled and then added to soups or deep-fried.

Xiao Long Bao: The word "xiao long" refers to the small bamboo steamer baskets in which they are cooked. These originate from the Shanghai region of China and are called "soup dumplings" for the filling that yields a rich, flavorful soup.

Your Dumpling Tool Kit

Making dumplings at home requires proper tools and equipment. I'll cover the essentials here, as well as some nice-to-haves that make the process more efficient.

FOR MAKING WRAPPERS AND FILLINGS

Cutting boards: One cutting board for animal proteins and another for vegetables and fruits to avoid cross-contamination; choose wood composite or plastic boards that are sturdy and have a wide surface but can fit in your dishwasher.

Knives: An all-purpose chef's knife and a paring knife work fine.

Measuring cups and spoons: Keep a standard measuring cup and spoon set handy. Pay attention to what the amounts look like when you measure them, so you can begin eyeballing your amounts for faster prep.

Mixing bowls: At least two mixing bowls—one for the dumpling dough and another for the filling; metal bowls are lighter to lift than glass or ceramic and can cool the filling faster.

Plastic scraper: A thin, flexible plastic baker's scraper comes in handy when turning out your dumpling dough from the bowl to the counter to knead it smooth. The scraper is also rigid enough to cut the dough into small pieces.

Prep bowls: Small reusable bowls that range from ¼ cup to 2 cups in size for holding measured ingredients.

Small rolling pin or dowel: When rolling out dumpling wrappers, the smaller the rolling pin, the more control you have. A thick wooden dowel a little wider than the width of your hand is ideal.

Strainer or colander: Keep one small wire-mesh strainer for sifting lumpy flour and one large strainer to drain canned goods or salted cabbage. A colander is helpful to drain washed greens.

Whisk and wooden spoon: The best tools for mixing doughs and fillings are your hands, but a whisk is helpful to incorporate dry ingredients for a dough, as is a wooden spoon to mix it all together.

FOR COOKING YOUR DUMPLINGS

Chopsticks: Chopsticks are great for lifting delicately steamed dumplings from their baskets, eating, and for general use. If you don't have chopsticks, tongs work just as well.

Large saucepan: For making soups and sauces, you'll need a saucepan large enough to hold 3 to 4 quarts.

Nonstick skillet with lid: This is a must-have for cooking potstickers and shengjian bao. A nonstick surface will keep the dumplings from sticking, and the lid will trap the steam. If you are concerned about nonstick material, consider choosing pans made from ceramic titanium, such as Scanpan.

Spatula: A thin, flexible metal spatula can easily slip underneath an unruly potsticker and unstick it; however, if your nonstick pan is coated, choose a silicone spatula to prevent scratching the pan.

Spider: Also called a skimmer, a wide mesh spider is an essential tool for lifting deep-fried dumplings from hot oil and transferring boiled wontons from their cooking water into soups. In a pinch, a slotted spoon works, too.

Steamer baskets: Classic stacking bamboo steamer baskets that come with a lid are inexpensive and handy—and not just for steaming dumplings. These baskets are made to fit over woks, but they can perch over a stockpot, if necessary, if the pot is wide enough for the baskets to sit and create a tight seal. Rinse the baskets under warm water before steaming so they do not absorb too much steam while cooking. An expandable metal blossom steamer basket is perfectly fine for steaming dumplings, too.

Wide stockpot with lid or a Dutch oven: The stockpot should be wide enough for the bamboo steamer basket to sit atop it, and deep enough to hold 6 to 8 quarts of water for boiling and steaming or oil for deep-frying.

NICE-TO-HAVES

Baking sheets and wire cooling racks: When deep-frying dumplings, I like to lift them out of the oil and set them onto a wire rack set over a baking sheet to drain.

Food processor: Some dough and filling recipes call for a food processor to mix them. You can certainly achieve the final product by hand, but a food processor can save you time. The only downside is having to clean it.

Instant-read thermometer: If you are concerned about food safety, use an instant-read thermometer to check the internal temperature of your filling, especially when cooking raw ground meat. The cooked temperature should read 165°F (74°C). A thermometer can also read the correct temperature of frying oil when setting up for deep-frying dumplings.

Kitchen scale: The Master Dough recipes feature both volume and weight measurements, so if you have a scale, by all means use it. Some cooks prefer to weigh the dough and fillings to maintain exact portions, too.

Portion scoop, #70: A commercial #70 scoop yields 70 portions from a quart of product. This size roughly translates to a generous tablespoon, which is a common amount of dumpling filling.

Tortilla press: If you have trouble manipulating the dough rolling it by hand, a tortilla press can be a helpful alternative.

Wok: Choose a lightweight carbon steel or nonstick 12-inch wok and make sure to get a tight-fitting lid. Scanpan makes the most fantastic nonstick woks I have ever used.

Your Dumpling Pantry

A well-stocked pantry is key to cooking dumplings. The good news is that many of the ingredients used are staples that can last quite a while in the refrigerator or cupboard.

DOUGHS AND WRAPPERS

Active dry yeast: A leavening agent for bao dough; store in an airtight container in the freezer.

All-purpose flour: Choose unbleached flour for basic dumpling wrappers.

Baking powder: Added to bao dough for extra fluffiness.

Cake flour: Low in protein and bleached, this finely-milled flour gives the steamed baos their bright white color and fluffy, cake-like texture.

Store-bought dumpling wrappers: Round in shape, they are slightly thicker than wonton wrappers and can be used for virtually any dumpling, like potstickers, gyoza, and even shu mai. Look for them in the refrigerated section of your local supermarket, usually near the tofu.

Store-bought wonton wrappers: It's hard to make wonton wrappers from scratch at home and get the paper-thin sheets without a pasta roller. Square-shaped store-bought wrappers can be great time-savers for wontons and parcel-folded dumplings, such as crab rangoon. Choose thin wrappers for boiled wontons, medium and thick wonton wrappers for steamed and deep-fried dumplings.

Sweet potato flour: The main ingredient in crystal dumpling dough, this turns from opaque white to translucent when cooked. In a pinch, potato starch or wheat starch works as a substitute.

Tapioca starch: Extracted from the cassava root, this starch makes crystal dumpling dough more pliable. A little goes a long way, so buy a small amount.

FILLINGS

Bamboo shoots: Young and tender bamboo shoots have a soft texture, like green beans, and a mild flavor, like celery. Like water chestnuts, they can be found fresh seasonally at many Asian markets and canned ones, whole or sliced, are available at most conventional grocery stores.

Cabbage: In dumpling fillings, cabbage is lightly salted to remove as much water as possible to improve its flavor and texture. Napa cabbage, softer in texture and milder in flavor than regular cabbage, is another good option. Use the broad outer leaves to line the bottoms of steamer baskets when cooking dumplings.

Chinese five-spice powder: A classic ground spice blend of star anise, cinnamon, cloves, fennel seeds, and Sichuan peppercorns, five-spice gives a pleasant warming sensation without being too "spicy."

Curry powder: A little bit of this spice blend goes a long way; choose mild or hot to your liking.

Ground chicken, pork, or turkey: Ground (or minced) meat is an ingredient in traditional dumpling fillings.

Mushrooms: When cooked down to remove water content, chopped mushrooms stand in nicely for ground meat. Dried shiitake mushrooms can be rehydrated in hot water, or processed to a fine powder to add more umami flavor.

Shrimp: Another popular filling ingredient, shrimp can be combined with ground meat. Shu mai uses small amounts of ground dried baby shrimp in the filling to provide a savory base.

Sichuan peppercorns: These are actually seeds from trees grown in China's Sichuan province. Their slight lemony flavor creates a tingling sensation in your mouth.

Spinach: Dark greens provide great color and texture to fillings. Wilt and squeeze the spinach as dry as possible before chopping and adding it to the filling.

Water chestnuts: These starchy nuggets are tender but crunchy. If you can't find fresh ones, canned versions already peeled and sliced work fine.

White pepper: Adding white pepper to fillings avoids marring the dish's aesthetics with black pepper flecks. It also gives a more earthy flavor than the basic heat of black pepper. White peppercorns are the same as black peppercorns, except that white ones are soaked and have their outer husks removed.

SEASONINGS, SAUCES, AND ACCOMPANIMENTS

Black bean sauce: Popular for stir-fry recipes, black bean sauce can instantly transform a simple dumpling filling by adding more flavor.

Black vinegar (Chinkiang): A rich, dark rice vinegar like aged balsamic vinegar; used in dipping sauces and marinades to lend an acidic balance.

Hoisin sauce: Hoisin is a sweet and salty soybean and chili sauce used often as an ingredient in fillings.

Kimchi: A spiced, fermented cabbage condiment from Korean cuisine is an essential ingredient in kimchi mandu. Keep a jar in your refrigerator. It keeps for months and can be added to virtually anything to enhance flavor (eggs, noodles, steamed rice, etc.).

Oyster sauce: Made from fermented oyster extract/flavoring, this dark, thick sauce is full of umami flavor. You can find vegetarian oyster-free versions of this sauce, if you prefer.

Salted mustard greens: These greens add a nice contrast to rich, fatty fillings, such as the one you might find in pork wontons.

Sesame oil: The nutty aroma and flavor of sesame oil boosts overall flavor and adds richness to your dumpling filling.

Shaoxing rice wine: Fermented rice wine with a low alcohol content (look for 15 to 16 percent ABV) adds depth of flavor to fillings, especially those with ground meat. Double-check the label for no more than 1.5 percent salt. Salt increases shelf life. Dry sherry can be used as a substitute.

Soy sauce: Use Chinese-style soy in Chinese recipes and Japanese-style soy in Japanese recipes. In Chinese cooking there are three types of soy sauce: light (thinner, lighter, and saltier), dark (deeper flavor and less salty), and a mushroom-flavored soy that adds an umami punch.

The Steps to Dumpling Success

In this section, I'll give a brief overview of the dumpling-making process. We'll take a deeper dive into dough making and shaping wrappers later, in chapter 2. You'll find that making dumplings doesn't have to be an all-in-one go. Here, I point out where you can break up the steps over a few days. In fact, some fillings develop better flavor and texture when left to sit for a day or two.

MAKE YOUR DOUGH

If you can stir together flour and water, you can make dumpling dough from scratch! Before we go through making your own wrappers in chapter 2, it's good to have a high-level understanding of the major steps.

Mixing the dough generally involves stirring together the dry and wet ingredients. As soon as the mixture forms a shaggy mass, you'll start kneading it until it turns into a smooth ball, which takes 4 to 5 minutes. Resting allows the dough to relax and loosen, making it stretchier and more pliable, before rolling and shaping the dough into wrappers.

After resting, you can cut the dough into small equal pieces, then roll each piece into flat, round wrappers. Keep the dough and wrappers covered with plastic wrap as much as possible. Overall, the entire process to prepare the wrappers takes about 45 minutes.

MAKE YOUR FILLING

For fillings, my best advice is to have all the ingredients measured before you start. Some fillings, at the start of the process, require 20 to 30 minutes of downtime (like salting cabbage), so get that going first. Finish the remaining prep while you wait.

When making meat-based fillings, thoroughly mix the filling until it begins to look like a thick paste. When squeezed in the palm of your hand, the filling mixture should hold together without falling apart. Many fillings benefit from 30 minutes of chilling in the refrigerator, or up to two days, if covered tightly. Chilling helps the flavors develop and improves the texture of the proteins. This makes dumplings tender and juicy when cooked.

You can make the filling a couple days ahead, and if necessary, you can also freeze it. Seal the raw filling in gallon-size heavy-duty resealable bags, flatten, and freeze in a single layer.

PORTION AND SHAPE YOUR WRAPPERS

After the dough rests, portion and roll out the wrappers. There are two methods for portioning—figure out which one works best for you. The first method involves a kitchen scale: weigh the dough and divide the total weight into 24 equal balls. The second method is less exact: divide the dough into two equal pieces. Roll each piece into a log 8 inches long, about 1½ inches thick. Cut the logs into 12 equal pieces and roll each piece into a ball. Keep the balls covered with plastic wrap until you are ready to roll the wrappers.

To roll out the wrappers, a short wooden dowel or rolling pin is the best tool; however, flattening crystal dough using a tortilla press is a great way to get kids to help. Keep the wrappers covered with plastic wrap to prevent them from drying out.

When first starting out, roll out six wrappers at a time, then fill and fold the dumplings. Wrappers become dry and brittle and will be difficult to pleat the longer they sit out. If you have friends and family helping, set up an assembly line: form wrappers, then fill, then fold.

FILL AND FOLD YOUR DUMPLINGS

When filling dumplings, less is more. Overfilling leads to burst dumplings when they're cooked. When placing filling in the wrapper, aim for the center of the wrapper and slightly flatten and spread the filling, leaving at least ¼-inch of space around the edges for sealing.

A good way to fill dumplings is to lay out the wrappers and then portion the filling into them all at once. This way, you can focus on placing an equal amount of filling on each wrapper. Each dumpling recipe offers guidance on how much filling to place on a wrapper, but a generous tablespoon is more than enough.

Folding dumplings takes practice. Restaurant workers fold hundreds of dumplings in one shift so muscle memory eventually takes over. You, too, will get better at it the more you do it. Even if you have a hard time making decent-looking pleats, as long as you get the entire wrapper to seal around the filling so nothing leaks out, you're good to go. My special trick is to pinch and seal tightly with my thumb and index finger, using a small dab of cornstarch slurry if the wrapper edges feel too dry.

HOW TO STORE YOUR DUMPLINGS

If you are not planning to cook your freshly folded dumplings right away, store them on a baking sheet lined with parchment or wax paper and tightly wrapped with plastic wrap. They will keep in the refrigerator for up to two days.

A word on large batches of dumplings: when making multiple batches, keep your filling in the refrigerator and work with small portions at a time to keep the filling from becoming too warm. Move batches of folded dumplings into the refrigerator while you continue to fold. Don't let the raw dumplings sit out at room temperature for more than two hours before storing them properly or cooking them.

STOCK YOUR FREEZER

The best thing about making multiple batches of dumplings is you can freeze them to have a stash of dumplings ready to go. You'll have delicious dumplings in minutes without having to make them from scratch.

You can also freeze dumpling components ahead of time, such as dumpling wrappers, fillings, stocks, and soups.

Wontons and dumplings made with basic dumpling wrappers can be frozen raw, then cooked from frozen. Steamed baos and crystal dumplings are best frozen after cooking, then reheated. You can also freeze Basic Dumpling Dough (page 20) wrappers on their own, as long as they are prerolled and stacked with wax paper between them. Wrap tightly in plastic wrap and make sure you label and date the package.

TO FREEZE DUMPLINGS

▸ Lay them on a baking sheet lined with parchment or wax paper. Make sure they do not touch.

▸ Wrap them tightly with plastic wrap and chill in the refrigerator for 1 hour, then move to the freezer overnight.

▸ Transfer the frozen dumplings to an airtight container or bag. Label and date the container.

▸ Frozen dumplings will last in the freezer for one to two months.

▸ Frozen dumplings should be boiled, steamed, or pan-fried from frozen—do not let them thaw. Just give them a few extra minutes to cook.

One caveat when cooking frozen dumplings: do not deep-fry them! Instead, fry the freshly made dumplings, then cool to room temperature before freezing. Reheat them on a sheet pan in a 350°F oven until heated through and crispy.

DUMPLING	FREEZE RAW OR COOKED?	HOW LONG WILL THEY KEEP?	HOW TO REHEAT/COOK
BAO	Cooked	2 to 3 months	Steam to reheat
BOILED OR STEAMED (JIAOZI, MANDU, XIAO LONG BAO)	Raw	1 to 2 months	Cook from frozen
CRYSTAL DUMPLING	Cooked	1 month	Reheat from frozen
PAN-FRIED (GYOZA, POTSTICKERS)	Raw	1 month	Cook from frozen
SHU MAI	Raw	1 to 2 months	Cook from frozen
WONTONS	Raw	1 to 2 months	Boil from frozen

Dumpling Cooking Techniques

In this section, we'll cover four dumpling cooking techniques, each yielding a different texture. I'll also teach you which dumplings can be cooked multiple ways.

BOILING

The simplest way to cook dumplings at home is to boil them in seasoned water. When paired with a flavorful sauce or condiment, like chili oil or vinegar, boiled dumplings are perfectly balanced with a tender but chewy exterior and a juicy filling. Added to a flavorful broth, boiled dumplings can also make a hearty soup.

Wontons and any dumplings made with Basic Dumpling Dough (page 20) can be boiled—just make sure the filling is sealed tightly with no gaps in the dough!

STEAMING

Steamed dumplings come in a variety of shapes and sizes: translucent crystal dumplings like har gow, cup-shaped shu mai, fluffy char siu bao, and many other delicious combinations of fillings folded into interesting shapes.

Steaming is a fast cooking process. Many recipes take just a few minutes to cook through. As with boiling, no oil is used, so the only flavor comes from the filling. You don't need a bamboo steamer, but you'll need at least a stockpot, steamer basket, and lid. Serve steamed dumplings with a flavorful sauce or condiment.

PAN-FRYING

This method is a combination of steaming and pan-frying. First, the dumplings are briefly fried to develop a light crust on their bottoms, then a small amount of water is added to the pan. The pan is covered, and the steam cooks the dumplings. Finally, the lid is lifted, and any residual water is allowed to evaporate; during this process the bottoms become deep brown and crispy.

Potstickers, gyoza, and shengjian bao are the most common pan-fried dumplings, but nearly any dumpling made from Basic Dumpling Dough (page 20) or Bao Dough (page 22) can be pan-fried. Serve the dumplings crispy-bottom up!

DEEP-FRYING

The magic of a deep-fried dumpling! Its golden, crunchy exterior makes it easy to pop one straight into your mouth, so it makes the perfect finger food for parties.

Deep-fried dumplings are best for those dumplings made with wonton skins, Basic Dumpling Dough (page 20) wrappers, and Crystal Dumpling Dough (page 21). Make sure the filling doesn't have excess moisture, as the dumplings tend to explode from the steam expanding in the filling as they cook.

Troubleshooting Your Dumplings

How many dumplings should I serve per person?

Generally, serving three to four different types of dumpling, with two of each type per person, makes a satisfying meal. Serve a platter of noodles or sautéed vegetables on the side to round out the meal.

How do I stop my dumplings from unraveling/bursting when I cook them?

The trick is to seal them well and to make sure there are no holes or gaps where the filling can seep out, or the wrappers can fall apart. To prevent bursting, squeeze out as much excess moisture from wet filling ingredients as possible before mixing into the filling.

My frozen dumpling skins are cracked. How do I rescue them?

Sadly, there isn't much that can be done if frozen dumpling skins are cracked—it's a form of freezer burn, where the wrapper loses too much moisture to the freezer environment. If you have fresh dumpling wrappers, you can rescue the filling and place them into fresh skins. To avoid cracked dumplings, don't keep them in the freezer for more than one to two months. And chill the fresh dumplings in the refrigerator for an hour before moving them to the freezer.

How can I make sure my filling is seasoned correctly before I fold a bunch of dumplings?

Taste test your filling by cooking a small meatball-size patty in a skillet. After you've tasted the cooked filling, you can decide if you need to add more salt or other seasonings.

Help! My dumplings clump together/stick to the pan when I cook them.

If the dumplings stick together during cooking, that's a sign they didn't have enough room around them when cooking and were too crowded in the pan. Add more water to the pan to steam them, then carefully pry them apart. If they stuck together while boiling, there wasn't enough water in the pot. Try boiling them again in fresh water and pull them apart gently. If your potstickers are stuck to the pan, add more oil to the pan and tilt the pan to slip the oil underneath the dumplings. Turn off the heat and let the dumplings rest for a few moments. Sometimes, potstickers will contract and unstick themselves. A very thin, flexible metal spatula, like a fish turner, can also slip underneath and dislodge them.

How can I tell when the dumplings are cooked?

Boiled dumplings may float before they are fully cooked. Recipes that include raw ground meat in the filling call for boiling the dumplings, then adding cold water to bring the temperature down, then boiling the cooking water at least twice to ensure the filling is cooked through. To make sure, sacrifice one dumpling and insert the probe of an instant-read thermometer into its thickest part. A fully cooked filling should be at least 165°F (74°C).

How to Use the Recipes

The recipes in this book focus on the most popular and beginner-friendly dumplings. Once you've mastered these recipes, experiment with more creative fillings and doughs. Start with the basic half-moon fold, or the wonton fold, before moving on to the more intricate pleated crescent or xiao long bao fold.

Chapter 2 includes three Master Dough recipes and folding instructions for five different classic dumpling shapes, including my favorite, the parcel fold! Chapters 3, 4, and 5 include instructions for making the fillings, plus cooking instructions for boiled, steamed, and pan-fried dumplings. Each recipe in chapters 3, 4, and 5 calls for one of the Master Dough recipes and one of the folding instructions provided in chapter 2. Chapter 6 covers soups, sauces, and other dumpling accompaniments.

Each dumpling recipe also features Cooking Tips to help with preparation. Make It Easier tips offer ideas for saving time or effort, and Mix It Up tips show you how to create new versions of a classic dumpling.

My hope is that this book will help you feel confident making dumplings at home. Pick your favorite dumpling and cook it several times to master it. Make notes on the pages to remind yourself what worked, and what you want to do differently next time. I hope you enjoy making dumplings at home and delight your friends and family with your new skills and creations!

2

A STEP-BY-STEP GUIDE TO DOUGHS AND FOLDS

If you think making dumplings is too difficult, I have news for you. Wrappers are easier to make than you think. But it's totally fine to use store-bought wrappers, too. In fact, there's nothing wrong with using premade wrappers, especially if you're making your own filling and folding them yourself!

In this chapter, I'll show you how to make dumpling dough from scratch and how to create the most common dumpling folds. Let's get started!

A Dumpling Dough Primer

This section covers the different types of dumpling doughs as well as their shapes and sizes. I'll also introduce five easy folds that you'll use to make the dumplings in this book.

STORE-BOUGHT VERSUS HOMEMADE

The ongoing debate over store-bought versus homemade wrappers rages on. Let me share the merits of each, so you can decide for yourself.

Store-bought wrappers are time-saving, convenient, and uniform in size and thickness, but they aren't as easy to pleat as homemade wrappers. And, depending on where you live, there may be limited choices available.

Homemade wrappers can elevate your dumpling quality and you can add flavoring elements to customize them. They are inexpensive to make, and when you roll them out, the edges get thinner than the center, which makes pleating them easier. The only drawback is time: the dough must rest before you can roll each wrapper to size.

Unless you need to make a dumpling like har gow, which requires the crystal dumpling wrapper—which must be made from scratch—you can use store-bought wrappers for most dumplings in this book.

TYPES OF DOUGH

There are as many kinds of dough for equally as many types of dumplings; however, this book covers the three main wrappers, or what we call Master Recipes.

Basic dumpling dough. This is the main, all-purpose wrapper you can make if you decide to forego the store-bought varieties.

Crystal dumpling dough. When cooked, this wrapper turns translucent, showing the filling inside. Though it's mainly used for steamed shrimp dumplings like har gow, I've seen crystal wrappers used for colorful vegetable fillings for maximum visual impact.

Bao dough. Used for most of the steamed buns (or baos), this yeasted dough yields a soft, fluffy texture that is more cake-like than a burger bun.

You can customize each dough to suit your style and tastes, adding spices and vegetable powders to create new flavors and colors.

WRAPPER SIZES AND SHAPES

Every dumpling starts out with either a round or square wrapper. But it's the folding of the wrapper that determines the final shape of the dumpling.

The thickness of the wrapper determines the texture of the cooked dumpling. For instance, wontons generally require paper-thin square wrappers to create a soft, slippery texture, whereas potstickers use thicker round wrappers for a chewier texture.

Experimenting with different wrappers is the best (and most delicious) way to determine which shape and thickness is most appropriate. When eating out, order a variety of dumplings and pay attention to their folds, shapes, and the thickness of the wrappers. Take photos for reference and recreate them at home. The best part is, you get to eat your practice dumplings!

WORKING WITH STORE-BOUGHT WRAPPERS

As Ina Garten says, "store-bought is fine!" I agree with her wholeheartedly when it comes to wrappers. Here are some tips for success when working with store-bought wrappers:

▸ Keep the wrappers refrigerated and use them within five days of purchase.

▸ The wrappers might be drier than homemade ones. Lightly mist with water from a spray bottle, then blot with a paper towel. Or, remove from the packaging and wrap the wrappers in damp paper towels for about 30 minutes before using.

▸ Make the wrappers thinner by rolling them out with a small dowel or rolling pin. Trim to original size with a round cutter or paring knife.

▸ The drier the wrapper, the more difficult it will be to pleat and seal the dumpling. Mix 1 teaspoon (3 g) cornstarch with 1 tablespoon (15 g) warm water and moisten the edges of the wrapper using your finger dipped in the slurry before pleating. This will help glue the edges together.

Master Dough #1
BASIC DUMPLING DOUGH

MAKES 24 dumplings **ACTIVE TIME** 10 minutes **REST TIME** 40 minutes, or up to 2 hours

Here is the all-purpose dumpling wrapper you will use for potstickers, gyoza, and boiled, steamed, or fried dumplings. You only need all-purpose flour, a pinch of salt, and some water! Play around with the thickness of the wrapper for different textures.

1½ cups (187 g) all-purpose flour

⅛ teaspoon kosher salt

½ cup plus 1 tablespoon (255 g) warm water

1. In a mixing bowl, stir together the flour and salt.

2. Slowly pour in the water and mix to combine with a wooden spoon. Stir until a shaggy dough mass forms.

3. Transfer the dough to a clean work surface and knead it for 4 to 5 minutes until the dough is smooth and supple.

4. Wrap the dough in plastic wrap and let the dough rest at room temperature for at least 40 minutes, or up to 2 hours, before cutting and rolling into wrappers.

Master Dough #2
CRYSTAL DUMPLING DOUGH

MAKES 24 dumplings **ACTIVE TIME** 15 minutes **REST TIME** up to 1 hour

Crystal dough is the translucent wrapper used specifically for Har Gow (page 55) and Crystal Chive Dumplings (page 63) to let the delicious filling peek through the wrapper. Thanks to the sweet potato starch, the uncooked wrapper looks opaque, but it changes consistency and texture as it steams. For a pop of color, add ½ teaspoon beet powder or ground turmeric to the dough.

¾ cup (96 g) sweet potato starch

⅓ cup (40 g) tapioca starch

⅛ teaspoon kosher salt

1 cup (240 g) hot water, just boiled

1 tablespoon (14 g) canola oil

Cornstarch, for dusting

1. In a mixing bowl, stir together the sweet potato starch, tapioca starch, and salt.

2. Pour the hot water over the starch mixture and stir together until just combined. The mixture will look rough and shaggy with some dry spots.

3. Cover the bowl with plastic wrap and let rest for 10 minutes. This allows the dough time to absorb the water and for the steam from the hot water to develop the dough's texture.

4. Add the oil and mix the dough until it becomes crumbly.

5. Transfer the dough to a clean work surface and knead the dough with your hands for 4 to 5 minutes, or until smooth. If the dough seems a bit sticky, dust your hands with cornstarch and keep kneading.

6. Wrap the dough in plastic wrap and let rest at room temperature for up to 1 hour, covered with a towel to keep it warm, so it is pliable for folding.

Master Dough #3
BAO DOUGH

MAKES 24 buns **ACTIVE TIME** 15 minutes **REST TIME** 1 hour for starter,
plus 1 hour to proof

Soft, white, and fluffy, this bao dough can be used for steamed buns like the Char Siu Bao (page 54) and pan-fried buns such as Shengjian Bao (page 75). The key ingredient here is cake flour, which creates a soft, tender crumb.

FOR THE STARTER

1 cup (240 g) luke-warm water

½ cup (100 g) sugar

2 teaspoons (6 g) active dry yeast

1½ cups (195 g) cake flour

FOR THE DOUGH

1 tablespoon (15 g) rice vinegar

½ teaspoon (3 g) kosher salt

2 cups (240 g) cake flour, plus ¼ cup (30 g) for dusting

1 tablespoon (14 g) baking powder

¼ teaspoon (1 g) baking soda

1 tablespoon (14 g) unsalted butter, at room temperature

Nonstick cooking spray

1. **To make the starter:** In a large bowl, stir together the water, sugar, and yeast. Set aside for 10 minutes, or until the mixture starts to foam.

2. Stir in the cake flour until well mixed. Cover the bowl with plastic wrap and let the mixture rise in a warm place for 1 hour.

3. **To make the dough:** Stir the vinegar and salt into the starter. In another bowl, sift together 2 cups of cake flour, the baking powder, and baking soda.

4. Stir the flour mixture into the yeast mixture to combine. Add the butter, mixing it in with your fingers until the dough becomes a sticky, shaggy mass.

5. Dust a work surface with flour and transfer the dough to it. Knead the dough for about 5 minutes, or until smooth, sprinkling with more flour as necessary.

6. Coat the inside of a large bowl with cooking spray. Transfer the dough to the oiled bowl and cover it with a damp cloth or plastic wrap. Let it rise in a warm place for 1 hour.

7. Lightly push down the dough and knead it into a smooth ball. Keep the dough tightly wrapped in plastic wrap until ready to use. Do not let it sit at room temperature for more than 1 hour to avoid overproofing.

HOST A DUMPLING PARTY!

Many hands make light work, as the saying goes. Just as it's more fun to enjoy dumplings with friends and family, it's even more fun to get them in on the action by hosting a dumpling party! Best of all, having friends and family help assemble the dumplings means you can enjoy them that much faster.

TIPS FOR HOSTING A SUCCESSFUL DUMPLING PARTY

▸ Prepare all the fillings and wrappers ahead of time. Guests can help with rolling, filling, and pleating. It will go faster if you have everything prepared and ready to go for assembly. Har gow, steamed baos, and shu mai are always party favorites.

▸ The same goes for any dipping sauces, teas, and snacks. Have these prepared and ready to go.

▸ Keep the folding simple. Decide on two or three easy folds you can show others how to make, like the half-moon and parcel folds. Don't get too focused on how the dumplings turn out. As long as the dumpling is filled and wrapped and somewhat pleated, it will taste delicious!

▸ Set out multiple piles of wrappers, small bowls of filling, and several sets of tools and slurry so people aren't reaching over each other.

▸ Get creative! Set up a mixing station of proteins and filling ingredients and invite guests to create their own fillings.

▸ Avoid anything that requires deep-frying, as it can be unsafe if people aren't paying attention. Instead, make pan-fried dumplings, such as potstickers or shengjian bao.

Portioning and Rolling Out Your Wrappers

So, you've got your dumpling dough. Now, it's time to turn it into dumpling wrappers. Keep in mind, store-bought wrappers have way more than 24 in each package, whereas the dough recipes in this book yield about 24 wrappers. You can scale up the recipe if you need more than 24 dumplings.

The best place to start is by cutting your dough into 24 equal pieces. Let's walk through the steps:

1. Place the dough on a clean work surface. Using a knife or pastry bench scraper, cut the dough into two equal pieces. Wrap one half in plastic wrap and set aside.

2. Using the flat part of your palms, roll the dough into a 6-inch-long log, 1 to 1½ inches in diameter.

3. Using a knife or a bench scraper, halve the log crosswise. Then, halve each piece crosswise again to yield four equal pieces.

4. Cut each piece into thirds, making 12 equal pieces.

5. Roll each dough piece into a ball and place on a baking sheet. Cover with plastic wrap. Repeat the process with the reserved dough from step 1.

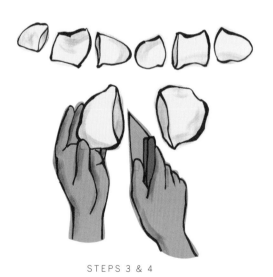

STEPS 3 & 4

STEP 5

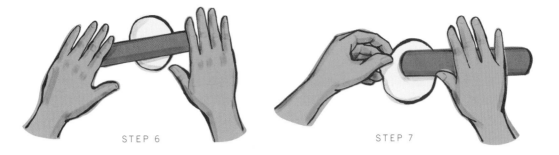

STEP 6   STEP 7

6. Flatten a dough ball with your fingertips, then use a rolling pin to roll it into a flat, thin disk, about ¼ inch thick.

7. Lift and rotate the disk 20 degrees clockwise. Then, roll the right side of the disk.

8. Keep lifting and rotating the dough as you roll it until the wrapper takes on a round shape and expands to 4 inches in diameter. The edges should be thinner than the center.

9. Repeat the rolling process with the remaining dough balls and keep the finished wrappers loosely covered with plastic wrap to prevent them from drying out. They can be loosely stacked on top of each other without sticking together.

The first time doing this, I recommend rolling out a few wrappers and then filling and folding them right away. The thin wrappers can dry out quickly, so rolling only a few at a time and keeping the balls covered with plastic wrap will help keep your wrappers moist and pliable.

Folding Techniques and Tips

Let's talk about folding the dumplings. The five folding techniques presented here represent the most popular dumpling shapes you can easily make at home. You'll learn basic folds like the half-moon, classic shapes like the wonton fold and pleated crescent for potstickers, and the box fold for a more contemporary look. We'll even cover the traditional soup dumpling fold. Even if you've never folded a dumpling, I'll show you, step-by-step, how to get the most authentic and delicious results.

Here are some tips for dumpling folding success:

Keep fillings chilled. Use a small bowl of filling when making dumplings and refill it from the main bowl in the refrigerator when you run out. Keep your filling chilled as much as possible until the dumplings are ready to be cooked. The proteins will also keep their shape better when cold.

Less is more. Overfilling makes it difficult to fold the dumplings. Use less filling than you think you need to get the shape down first. Once you've gotten the hang of folding them, you can gradually increase the amount of filling in the dumplings.

Practice makes perfect. Fold and pleat using your dominant hand while holding the wrapper steady in your other hand.

Prep your wrappers. To prevent dry wrappers, keep them under plastic wrap or under a damp cloth. A light dusting of rice flour or cornstarch between the wrappers can help keep them from sticking together.

Seal the deal. Close your dumplings tightly, so the fillings don't seep out during cooking. If you are using store-bought wrappers, use my magic sealing solution (see below) to help glue the pleats and folds together. It's basically a cornstarch slurry, but you can also use water or egg whites to help seal the edges.

Fold #1: The Basic Half-Moon Fold

This is the easiest shape for boiled or steamed dumplings. You can make a variation of this fold using a square wrapper to make a triangle fold.

1. If using store-bought wrappers, in a small bowl, stir together 1 teaspoon (3 g) cornstarch and 1 tablespoon (15 g) warm water to create a cornstarch slurry. Skip the slurry if using homemade wrappers. The slurry helps store-bought wrappers stick together to seal (they have a drier consistency than homemade ones).

2. Lay 1 round wrapper on a cutting board and place 1 tablespoon (weight varies) of filling in the center. Use the back of the spoon to flatten the filling slightly.

3. If using store-bought wrappers, dip the tip of your index finger into the slurry and moisten the edge of the wrapper all the way around, re-dipping as necessary.

4. Fold the bottom edge of the wrapper up over the filling to meet the top edge and press at the top center to seal it. Press down the sides and pay attention to sealing the corners well, so the filling doesn't leak out. If some of the filling squeezes out as you seal the wrapper, open the wrapper and carefully remove some of the filling.

5. Place the sealed dumpling on a baking sheet and cover with plastic wrap. Repeat the process with the remaining filling and wrappers.

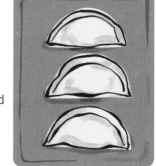

STEP 5

Fold #2: The Pleated Crescent Fold

This shape is the most common and recognizable fold for many Asian dumplings, and it is typically used for gyoza, har gow, and potstickers.

1. If using store-bought wrappers, in a small bowl, stir together 1 teaspoon (3 g) cornstarch and 1 tablespoon (15 g) warm water to create a cornstarch slurry. Skip the slurry if using homemade wrappers. The slurry helps store-bought wrappers stick together to seal (they have a drier consistency than homemade ones).

2. Lay 1 round wrapper on a cutting board and place 1 tablespoon (weight varies) of filling in the center. Use the back of the spoon to flatten the filling slightly.

3. If using store-bought wrappers, dip the tip of your index finger into the slurry and moisten the edge of the wrapper all the way around.

4. Pick up the top edge of the wrapper and, working from left to right, make 5 to 7 overlapping pleats across the edge, keeping the pleats as close together as possible.

5. As the pleats form, you'll notice the wrapper begins to cup around the filling.

STEP 4   STEP 5

continues ▶

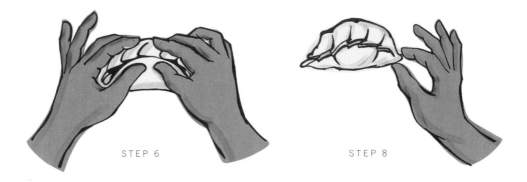

STEP 6   STEP 8

6. Bring up the bottom edge and line it up with the top edge of the pleats. Press the edges together and seal the corners so the filling doesn't leak out.

7. Holding the dumpling by the ridge of pleats on top, gently tap the dumpling on the board, creating a flat bottom. As you do this, use your fingers to help form a curved crescent. The dumpling should be standing straight up.

8. Place the finished dumpling on a baking sheet and cover with plastic wrap. Repeat the process with the remaining wrappers and filling.

Fold #3: The Classic Wonton Fold

This is the folding process for the classic wonton dumpling, whether it's boiled, then served in soup, or deep-fried.

1. If using store-bought wrappers, in a small bowl, stir together 1 teaspoon (3 g) cornstarch and 1 tablespoon (15 g) warm water to create a cornstarch slurry. Skip the slurry if using homemade wrappers. The slurry helps store-bought wrappers stick together to seal (they have a drier consistency than homemade ones).

2. Lay 1 square wrapper on a cutting board and place 1 tablespoon (weight varies) of filling in the center. Use the back of the spoon to flatten the filling slightly.

3. If using store-bought wrappers, dip the tip of your index finger into the slurry and moisten the edge of the wrapper around all four sides.

4. Lift the two opposite corners to meet, forming a triangle. Use your fingertips to seal the sides of the triangle while squeezing out as much air as possible.

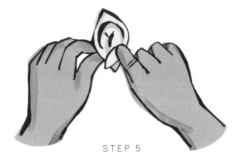

STEP 4

STEP 5

5. Pull the opposite two corners toward each other and crisscross them together. Pinch and seal where they meet as though you are making an X with the two ends. Use a dab of slurry to help keep them together, if needed.

6. Place the sealed dumpling on a plate and cover with plastic wrap. Repeat with the remaining wonton wrappers and filling.

Fold #4: The Parcel Fold

This is a more difficult fold but has a nice contemporary look when it's cooked. You see this shape more commonly with deep-fried dumplings such as Crab Rangoons (page 78).

1. If using store-bought wrappers, in a small bowl, stir together 1 teaspoon (3 g) cornstarch and 1 tablespoon (15 g) warm water to create a cornstarch slurry. Skip the slurry if using homemade wrappers. The slurry helps store-bought wrappers stick together to seal (they have a drier consistency than homemade ones).

2. Lay 1 square or round wrapper on a cutting board and place 1 tablespoon (weight varies) of filling in the center. Use the back of the spoon to flatten the filling slightly.

3. If using store-bought wrappers, dip the tip of your index finger into the slurry and moisten the edge of the wrapper around all four sides.

continues ▶

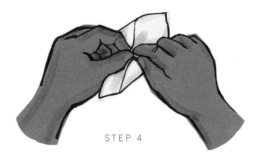

STEP 4

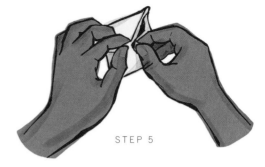

STEP 5

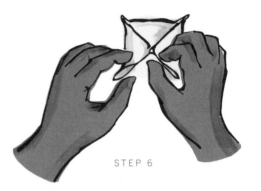

STEP 6

4. Bring two opposite edges of the wrapper together and pinch them together in the center.

5. Then, bring the other two opposite sides together and pinch in the center.

6. Pinch together each of the four "petals" to create an X, squeezing out any air from the dumpling before sealing the edges.

7. Transfer the sealed dumplings to a plate and cover with plastic wrap. Repeat with the remaining wrappers and filling.

Fold #5: Soup Dumpling Fold

Aside from the pleated crescent, the soup dumpling fold is the other most recognizable shape for classic dumplings such as Xiao Long Bao (page 52) or steamed momos. Typically, these dumplings are steamed and reveal a tender, juicy filling inside once cooked. You can use this folding method to create steamed baos as well. This fold starts out like the Pleated Crescent Fold (see page 27) but the pleating continues all the way around the edge of the wrapper, not just on one-half of the wrapper.

1. If using store-bought wrappers, in a small bowl, stir together 1 teaspoon (3 g) cornstarch and 1 tablespoon (15 g) warm water to create a cornstarch slurry. Skip the slurry if using homemade wrappers. The slurry helps store-bought wrappers stick together to seal (they have a drier consistency than homemade ones).

2. Lay 1 round wrapper on a cutting board and place 1 tablespoon (weight varies) of filling in the center. Use the back of the spoon to flatten the filling slightly.

3. If using store-bought wrappers, dip the tip of your index finger into the slurry and moisten the edge of the wrapper all the way around.

4. With your nondominant hand, pick up the wrapper and pinch the edge with your thumb and index finger at the 12 o'clock position. While cupping the dumpling in your palm, gently hold the top edge of the wrapper with your thumb and index finger.

5. Using your dominant thumb and index finger, hold the same edge 2 inches away from the place you're already holding it.

STEP 5

STEP 6

6. Gently stretch the wrapper a tiny bit with your free hand, then fold the stretched edge over itself, making a pleat. Pinch to seal.

7. Continue making pleats around the dumpling; the pleats will come together, forming a circle, and the wrapper will form a cup. It's okay if you have to stretch the wrapper a bit to keep pleating.

8. When you have completed pleating around the entire circumference of the wrapper, gather the pleated edges together and twist, pinching them into a little top knot. Grasp the top knot and lift the dumpling up, letting it suspend briefly to stretch the shape into a pouch. This helps create that classic soup dumpling shape when steamed.

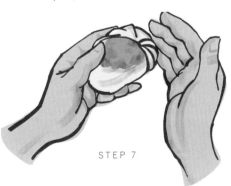

STEP 7

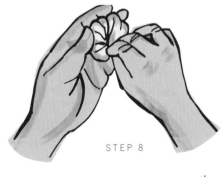

STEP 8

continues ▶

9. Set the dumpling in a steaming tray lined with Napa cabbage leaves and repeat the process with the remaining wrappers and filling.

10. To use this pleating method for steamed baos, press the bao dough into a 4-inch-wide circle, place the filling in the center, and make larger pleats all the way around. Gather up all the pleats to create a pouch. Gather the top and twist it into a knot. You don't have to create pleats for this bao—just bring up all the edges and twist into a top knot.

STEP 9

Troubleshooting Your Dough

Don't be discouraged if your dumplings aren't "restaurant quality" at first. Here are some troubleshooting tips and answers to the most common dumpling problems.

Can dumpling wrappers be made without flour for gluten-free options?
Absolutely! Try the Crystal Dumpling Dough (page 21), which is gluten-free; and use gluten-free baking mixes such as King Arthur's Measure for Measure flour instead of all-purpose flour for the Basic Dumpling Dough (page 20).

How thick should the dumpling wrapper be when rolled out properly?
When rolled out, the wrapper should be between 3 and 4 inches in diameter and have the same thickness as a tortilla. As you rotate and roll the wrapper, the edges will become thinner than the center of the wrapper, which is great because thinner edges make for easier pleating.

My dumpling dough seems stiff and dry. What can I do to fix that?
If the dough seems dry, perhaps a little more water is needed. As you knead, sprinkle some water on the surface.

Can I freeze the dumplings?
Absolutely! The best practice is to assemble the dumplings completely and freeze them on a baking sheet. Once they are frozen, transfer them to a resealable bag. Cook them from frozen—there is no need to defrost the frozen dumplings before cooking.

Can I freeze store-bought wrappers?
Yes, you can. Thaw them in the refrigerator for three to four days before using. They will be less pliable, but spray them lightly with water and roll them out a bit before using them.

What should I do if my dumpling wrappers tear?
You can repair small tears and holes by rolling out a very thin piece of another dumpling wrapper. Brush the slurry over the tear and patch it. Roll out the wrapper to smooth out the thickness.

I steamed my char siu baos in a bamboo steamer and they came out yellow. What happened?
Bamboo steamers, especially newer ones, give off a golden-colored steam, which will tint your dumplings. When cooking dumplings such as potstickers or har gow, you won't notice it much. However, the yeasted buns will take on the color much more. To avoid this, steam the buns in stainless-steel steamers instead.

Shui Jiao, page 36

3

BOILED DUMPLINGS

If you're new to making dumplings, start with the boiled dumplings in this chapter, like Shui Jiao (page 36) and Beef and Scallion Dumplings (page 41). Boiling is the simplest cooking method and ensures a tender, juicy filling. Many of the fillings you'll find here also work in the steamed or pan-fried dumplings in chapters 4 and 5. You can also change up the wrappers and folding methods to suit your taste.

SHUI JIAO

MAKES 24 dumplings **PREP TIME** 35 minutes **COOK TIME** 30 minutes

Shui jiao, or "water dumplings," are an everyday staple in many Chinese households. Shaped like half-moons and filled with pork and vegetables, these are tasty and hearty. Make an extra batch to keep in the freezer when you're short on time. They can be on the table in the time it takes to boil the water!

1 (10-ounce) package frozen spinach, defrosted, squeezed, and chopped

8 ounces ground pork

1 tablespoon light soy sauce

1 tablespoon Shaoxing rice wine

Pinch ground white pepper

2 tablespoons sesame oil

1/2-inch piece fresh ginger, peeled and minced

1 batch Basic Dumpling Dough (page 20), or 24 store-bought dumpling wrappers

1 tablespoon kosher salt

2 to 3 tablespoons Scallion-Ginger Oil (page 102), for garnish

MIX IT UP: *After boiling these dumplings, you can pan-fry them to add a crispy texture to the skins. Follow the pan-frying instructions in chapter 5 (see page 70).*

1. **Make the filling:** In a large bowl, stir together the spinach, ground pork, soy sauce, rice wine, and white pepper. Add the sesame oil and ginger and mix until thoroughly combined. Cover and refrigerate while you roll the dough, or up to 2 days.

2. **Roll out the wrappers and fold the dumplings:** Cut the dumpling dough into 24 pieces (see page 24). Roll each piece into a 4-inch circle about 1/16 inch thick around the edges. Keep covered.

3. Lay 6 wrappers on a cutting board and place 1 tablespoon of filling in the center of each. If using store-bought wrappers, moisten the outer edges of the wrapper with a cornstarch slurry (see page 26).

4. Fold the dumplings using the Basic Half-Moon Fold (see page 26). Repeat with the remaining wrappers and filling.

5. **Cook and serve:** In a medium stockpot, bring 8 cups of water to a boil and add the salt. Stir to dissolve. Add the dumplings, gently stirring to keep them from sticking. Bring the water back to a boil, then add 1 cup of cold water.

6. Bring the water to a boil again and cook the dumplings for 7 to 8 minutes. Reduce the heat and simmer the dumplings for 2 minutes, or until they float. Using a spider, transfer the dumplings to a warm platter.

7. Serve with the scallion-ginger oil.

TRADITIONAL SOUP WONTONS

SERVES 4 **PREP TIME** 35 minutes **COOK TIME** 20 minutes

With its comforting broth and soft, velvety texture, wonton soup always brings back child-hood memories. Mom and I had an agreement: if she needed me to help fold wontons, I'd fold them while watching Saturday morning cartoons.

8 ounces shrimp, peeled and deveined

1 (4-ounce) can sliced bamboo shoots, drained and chopped

½-inch piece fresh ginger, peeled and minced

2 teaspoons sesame oil

1 teaspoon light soy sauce

24 store-bought wonton wrappers

Cornstarch slurry (see page 26)

8 cups Wonton Soup Broth (page 90)

3 scallions, white and green parts, thinly sliced

MIX IT UP: *Add some variety and color to your soup by serving these with Tofu and Carrot Wontons (page 43).*

1. **Make the filling:** Roughly chop half the shrimp and set it aside. Finely chop the remaining shrimp, creating a shrimp paste, and place it in a medium bowl. Fold in the roughly chopped shrimp pieces. Add the bamboo shoots, ginger, sesame oil, and soy sauce. Gently stir together until thoroughly combined.

2. **Fold the dumplings:** While working, keep the wrappers covered. Lay 6 wrappers on a cutting board and place 1 tablespoon of filling in the center of each. Moisten the outer edge of the wrappers with cornstarch slurry.

3. Fold the dumplings using the Classic Wonton Fold (see page 28). Repeat with the remaining wrappers and filling.

4. **Cook and serve:** In a medium stockpot, bring the wonton broth to a boil, then reduce the heat to medium-high. Add the wontons and simmer for 3 to 4 minutes until cooked through, or until the wrappers turn translucent.

5. Divide the wontons and soup among warmed bowls and garnish with scallions. Cool for at least 1 minute, then serve.

SICHUAN WONTONS IN CHILI OIL

MAKES 24 dumplings **PREP TIME** 35 minutes **COOK TIME** 40 minutes

A popular Sichuan street food, these spicy wontons in chili oil are perfect for a winter night. The recipe also works great as an appetizer and helps prepare the palate for the main part of the meal.

12 small shrimp, peeled, deveined, and roughly chopped

8 ounces ground pork

3 garlic cloves, smashed

2 teaspoons light soy sauce

2 teaspoons Shaoxing rice wine

1/2 teaspoon freshly ground Sichuan peppercorns

1/2 teaspoon sugar

1/2 cup chili oil

2 tablespoons Chinkiang vinegar

24 store-bought wonton wrappers

Cornstarch slurry (see page 26)

1 tablespoon kosher salt

2 tablespoons roughly chopped fresh cilantro leaves

COOKING TIP: *If you can't find Chinkiang vinegar, substitute 2 tablespoons balsamic vinegar and 1 tablespoon rice vinegar.*

1. **Make the filling:** In a food processor, combine the shrimp, ground pork, garlic, soy sauce, rice wine, Sichuan pepper, and sugar. Pulse to form a smooth paste.

2. In a medium bowl, stir together the chili oil and vinegar and set aside.

3. **Fold the dumplings:** While working, keep the wrappers covered. Lay 6 wrappers on a cutting board and place 1 tablespoon of filling in the center of each. Moisten the outer edge of the wrappers with cornstarch slurry.

4. Fold the dumplings using the Classic Wonton Fold (see page 28). Repeat with the remaining wrappers and filling.

5. **Cook and serve:** In a medium stockpot, bring 8 cups of water to a boil and add the salt. Stir to dissolve.

6. Add the dumplings, gently stirring to keep them from sticking together. Bring the water to a boil again, cook the dumplings for 7 to 8 minutes, then add 1 cup of cold water. Bring the water to a boil again and cook the dumplings for 7 to 8 minutes more. Reduce the heat and simmer the dumplings for 2 minutes, or until they float. Using a skimmer, transfer the wontons to a warm serving bowl.

7. Stir 2 tablespoons of cooking water into the chili oil mixture and drizzle it over the dumplings. Garnish with cilantro to serve.

MANDU-GUK (KIMCHI DUMPLINGS IN EGG DROP SOUP)

SERVES 4 **PREP TIME** 35 minutes **COOK TIME** 35 minutes

Mandu-guk is a Korean-style dumpling soup served in a rich broth laced with egg. Traditionally eaten on New Year's Day, mandu-guk uses beef or anchovy broth, but this version uses vegetable stock.

1 medium zucchini, grated and squeezed of excess moisture

1 cup kimchi, drained and chopped

2 fresh shiitake mushrooms, stemmed and minced

1 tablespoon cornstarch

1 batch Basic Dumpling Dough (page 20), or 24 store-bought wonton wrappers

6 cups vegetable stock

3 large garlic cloves, smashed

2 tablespoons soy sauce

1 tablespoon sesame oil

½ teaspoon kosher salt

2 large eggs, lightly beaten

3 scallions, green parts only, sliced on the diagonal

1 teaspoon toasted sesame seeds

MAKE IT EASIER: *Since this recipe uses wonton folds, you can use store-bought wonton wrappers, if you prefer.*

1. **Make the filling:** In a large bowl, stir together the zucchini, kimchi, mushrooms, and cornstarch. Set aside.

2. **Roll out the wrappers and fold the dumplings:** Cut the dumpling dough into 24 pieces (see page 24). Roll each piece into a 3½-inch circle about 1/16 inch thick around the edges. Keep covered.

3. Lay 6 wrappers on a cutting board and place 1 tablespoon of filling in the center of each. If using store-bought wrappers, moisten the outer edges of the wrapper with cornstarch slurry (see page 26).

4. Fold the dumplings using the Classic Wonton Fold (see page 28). Repeat with the remaining wrappers and filling.

5. **Cook and serve:** In a large saucepan, combine the vegetable stock, garlic, soy sauce, sesame oil, and salt. Bring to a boil and cook for 8 to 10 minutes. Add the dumplings and return the liquid to a boil. Reduce the heat to low and simmer the dumplings for 5 to 8 minutes, or until they float.

6. Gently stir the soup and pour in the beaten eggs as you stir, creating ribbons of egg. Add the scallions and simmer for 30 seconds.

7. Divide the soup and dumplings among bowls. Top with sesame seeds to serve.

FISH AND NAPA CABBAGE DUMPLINGS

MAKES 24 dumplings **PREP TIME** 50 minutes **COOK TIME** 25 minutes

These dumplings have a delicate flavor thanks to the cod, but you can use any mild white fish, such as sole, pollock, or haddock. Use fish sauce in place of the rice wine for a richer flavor. Enjoy these dumplings with Scallion-Ginger Oil (page 102).

2 cups shredded Napa cabbage

2 tablespoons kosher salt, divided

8 ounces cod fillets, cut into small chunks

2 teaspoons Shaoxing rice wine

Ground white pepper

1 tablespoon cornstarch

1 scallion, white and green parts, minced

1 batch Basic Dumpling Dough (page 20) or 24 store-bought dumpling wrappers

MIX IT UP: *Serve with XO Sauce (page 100) for a deeper umami flavor.*

1. **Make the filling:** Wilt the cabbage with 1 tablespoon of salt for 10 to 15 minutes. Squeeze out the excess water, then transfer to a food processor.

2. Add the cod, rice wine, and a pinch of pepper to the food processor. Pulse until roughly chopped.

3. Add 2 tablespoons of water, the cornstarch, and scallion and pulse to form a smooth paste. Cover and refrigerate while you roll the dough, or up to 1 day.

4. **Roll out the wrappers and fold the dumplings:** Cut the dumpling dough into 24 pieces (see page 24). Roll each piece into a 4-inch circle about 1/16 inch thick around the edges. Keep covered.

5. Lay 6 wrappers on a cutting board and place 1 tablespoon of filling in the center of each. If using store-bought wrappers, moisten the outer edges of the wrapper with cornstarch slurry (see page 26).

6. Fold the dumplings using the Basic Half-Moon Fold (see page 26). Repeat with the remaining wrappers and filling.

7. **Cook and serve:** In a medium stockpot, bring 8 cups of water to a boil and add the remaining 1 tablespoon of salt. Stir to dissolve.

8. Add the dumplings and bring the water to a boil again, stirring occasionally. Reduce the heat to low and simmer the dumplings for 2 to 3 minutes, or until they float. Using a spider, transfer the dumplings to a warm platter.

BEEF AND SCALLION DUMPLINGS

MAKES 24 dumplings **PREP TIME** 40 minutes **COOK TIME** 40 minutes

This is a great starter recipe if you're new to making dumplings. These easy and satisfying dumplings pair well with just about any garnish you can dream up, but Chili Crisp Sauce (page 99) is especially nice.

12 ounces ground beef

1½ tablespoons light soy sauce

4 teaspoons sesame oil, divided

1 teaspoon grated peeled fresh ginger

⅛ teaspoon ground Sichuan peppercorns

¼ cup chicken stock

1 tablespoon cornstarch

5 or 6 scallions, white and green parts, thinly sliced, divided

1 batch Basic Dumpling Dough (page 20), or 24 store-bought dumpling wrappers

1 tablespoon kosher salt

MIX IT UP: *Substitute ground turkey for the beef. The dumplings will be just as tasty!*

1. **Make the filling:** In a food processor, combine the ground beef, soy sauce, 2 teaspoons of sesame oil, ginger, and Sichuan pepper and pulse to form a coarse paste. Add the chicken stock and cornstarch and pulse until well mixed.

2. Transfer the mixture to a large bowl and stir in half the scallions. Cover and refrigerate while you roll the dough, or up to 1 day.

3. **Roll out the wrappers and fold the dumplings:** Cut the dumpling dough into 24 pieces (see page 24). Roll each piece into a 4-inch circle about ¹⁄₁₆ inch thick around the edges. Keep covered.

4. Lay 6 wrappers on a cutting board, and place 1 tablespoon of filling in the center of each. If using store-bought wrappers, moisten the outer edges of the wrappers with cornstarch slurry (see page 26).

5. Fold using the Basic Half-Moon Fold (see page 26). Repeat with the remaining wrappers and filling.

6. **Cook and serve:** In a medium stockpot, bring 8 cups of water to a boil and add the salt. Stir to dissolve.

7. Add the dumplings, bring the water to a boil again, and cook for 7 to 8 minutes. Add 1 cup of cold water. Bring the water to a boil again and cook for 7 to 8 minutes. Reduce the heat and simmer for 2 minutes, or until floating. Using a spider, transfer the dumplings to a warm platter.

CHARRED CABBAGE AND CHIVE DUMPLINGS

MAKES 24 dumplings **PREP TIME** 30 minutes **COOK TIME** 25 minutes

Roasting cabbage until it chars around the edges gives it a deeper, richer flavor. Give this one a try—it's one of my favorites!

½ head green cabbage, cored and roughly chopped

4 fresh shiitake mushrooms, stemmed and sliced

2 garlic cloves, peeled

3 tablespoons vegetable oil

Pinch kosher salt, plus 1 tablespoon

¼ cup roughly chopped fresh Chinese garlic chives or scallions

1 tablespoon dark soy sauce or mushroom soy sauce

1 tablespoon cornstarch

2 teaspoons Shaoxing rice wine

2 teaspoons sesame oil

½ teaspoon sriracha sauce

1 batch Basic Dumpling Dough (page 20), or 24 store-bought dumpling wrappers

MIX IT UP: *Turn these dumplings into a delicious soup by adding them to a batch of Shiitake Mushroom Wonton Soup Broth (page 91).*

1. **Make the filling:** Preheat the oven to 450°F. Line a baking sheet with parchment paper.

2. On the baking sheet, toss together the cabbage, mushrooms, garlic, vegetable oil, and a pinch of salt. Roast for 15 to 25 minutes, or until the cabbage is charred around the edges. Remove from the oven and let cool.

3. Transfer to a food processor. Add the garlic chives, soy sauce, cornstarch, rice wine, sesame oil, and sriracha and pulse to form a thick paste. Transfer to a bowl and set aside.

4. **Roll out the wrappers and fold the dumplings:** Cut the dumpling dough into 24 pieces (see page 24). Roll each piece into a 4-inch circle about 1/16 inch thick around the edges. Keep covered.

5. Lay 6 wrappers on a cutting board and place 1 tablespoon of filling in the center of each. If using store-bought wrappers, moisten the outer edge of the wrappers with cornstarch slurry (see page 26).

6. Fold using the Pleated Crescent Fold (see page 27). Repeat with the remaining wrappers and filling.

7. **Cook and serve:** In a medium stockpot, bring 8 cups of water to a boil and add the remaining 1 tablespoon of salt. Stir to dissolve.

8. Add the dumplings, bring to a boil again, and cook the dumplings for 3 to 4 minutes. Reduce the heat and simmer the dumplings for 2 minutes, or until they float.

VEGAN

TOFU AND CARROT WONTONS

MAKES 24 wontons **PREP TIME** 1 hour 10 minutes **COOK TIME** 25 minutes

This plant-forward wonton is a lighter alternative to traditional wontons. Roasted carrots add sweetness and the hoisin sauce balances the Sichuan peppercorns for a satisfying flavor. Garnish with a drizzle of Chili Crisp Sauce (page 99) to serve.

5 or 6 medium carrots, cut into 2-inch chunks

3 garlic cloves, peeled

2 tablespoons vegetable oil

Pinch kosher salt, plus 1 tablespoon

4 ounces firm tofu, drained and cubed

½-inch piece fresh ginger, peeled and roughly chopped

1 tablespoon light soy sauce

2 teaspoons hoisin sauce

2 teaspoons sesame oil

¼ teaspoon ground Sichuan peppercorns

3 scallions, white and green parts, sliced

24 store-bought wonton wrappers

Cornstarch slurry (see page 26)

Chili Crisp Sauce (page 99), for serving

MAKE IT EASIER: *Use peeled baby carrots, if you're short on time.*

1. **Make the filling:** Preheat the oven to 425°F. Line a baking sheet with parchment paper.

2. On the prepared baking sheet, toss together the carrots, garlic, vegetable oil, and a pinch of salt. Roast for 15 to 25 minutes, or until browned and soft. Remove from the oven and let cool.

3. Transfer the carrots to a food processor. Add the tofu, ginger, soy sauce, hoisin, sesame oil, and Sichuan pepper. Pulse to form a smooth paste.

4. Transfer the mixture to a medium bowl and stir in the scallions. Set aside.

5. **Fold the dumplings:** While working, keep the wrappers covered. Lay 6 wrappers on a cutting board and place 1 tablespoon of filling in the center of each. Moisten the outer edges of the wrappers with cornstarch slurry.

6. Fold the wontons using the Classic Wonton Fold (see page 28). Repeat with the remaining wrappers and filling.

7. **Cook and serve:** In a medium stockpot, bring 8 cups of water to a boil and add the remaining 1 tablespoon of salt. Stir to dissolve.

8. Add the dumplings, bring the water to a boil again, and cook the dumplings for 3 to 4 minutes. Reduce the heat and simmer the dumplings for 2 minutes, or until they float. Using a spider, transfer the wontons to a warm platter.

VEGAN

MUSHROOM AND BAMBOO SHOOT DUMPLINGS

MAKES 24 dumplings **PREP TIME** 50 minutes, plus 30 minutes to cool
COOK TIME 25 minutes

This dumpling uses shiitake mushrooms for an earthy flavor and bamboo shoots for crunch. This recipe calls for shiitake and cremini mushrooms, but experiment with your favorite mushrooms. Use a vegetarian stir-fry sauce, like Lee Kum Kee's, which is a great alternative to oyster sauce.

VEGETARIAN

3 cups fresh shiitake mushrooms, stemmed and chopped

2 cups fresh cremini mushrooms, stemmed and chopped

1 (8-ounce) can bamboo shoots, drained and chopped

1 small shallot, chopped

½-inch piece fresh ginger, peeled and minced

3 tablespoons vegetable oil

2 tablespoons vegetarian stir-fry sauce

1 tablespoon sesame oil

2 tablespoons chopped fresh cilantro

1 batch Basic Dumpling Dough (page 20), or 24 store-bought dumpling wrappers

1 tablespoon kosher salt

MIX IT UP: *These dumplings make fantastic potstickers. Fry them using the potsticker cooking method (see page 70) instead of boiling.*

1. **Make the filling:** In a food processor, combine the shiitake and cremini mushrooms, bamboo shoots, shallot, and ginger and pulse to form a coarse paste.

2. In a large nonstick skillet over medium-high heat, heat the vegetable oil. Add the mushroom mixture, spread it into an even layer, and cook for 4 minutes, undisturbed. Stir and cook for 15 minutes more, or until most of the liquid has cooked off.

3. Stir in the stir-fry sauce and sesame oil and remove the skillet from the heat. Transfer the mixture to a medium bowl, fold in the cilantro, and set aside to cool for about 30 minutes.

4. **Roll out the wrappers and fold the dumplings:** Cut the dumpling dough into 24 pieces (see page 24). Roll each piece into a 4-inch circle about ¹⁄₁₆ inch thick around the edges. Keep covered.

5. Lay 6 wrappers on a cutting board and place 1 tablespoon of filling in the center of each. If using store-bought wrappers, moisten the outer edges of the wrappers with cornstarch slurry (see page 26).

6. Fold the dumplings using the Pleated Crescent Fold (see page 27). Repeat with the remaining wrappers and filling.

7. **Cook and serve:** In medium stockpot, bring 8 cups of water to a boil and add the salt. Stir to dissolve.

8. Add the dumplings, bring the water to a boil again, and cook the dumplings for 3 to 4 minutes. Reduce the heat and simmer the dumplings for 2 minutes, or until they float. Using a spider, gently transfer the dumplings to a warm platter.

TURKEY AND BLACK BEAN SAUCE DUMPLINGS

MAKES 24 dumplings **PREP TIME** 35 minutes **COOK TIME** 40 minutes

The umami flavor of this dumpling comes from the black bean sauce, a staple in every Chinese household pantry. A traditional filling would be made from ground pork. This recipe uses ground turkey for a lighter take on the classic filling.

5 ounces fresh baby spinach

⅔ pound ground turkey

½-inch piece fresh ginger, peeled and roughly chopped

2 teaspoons cornstarch

2 tablespoons black bean sauce

24 store-bought wonton wrappers

Cornstarch slurry (see page 26)

1 tablespoon kosher salt

2 tablespoons roughly chopped fresh cilantro leaves

COOKING TIP: *Leftover Thanksgiving turkey works great for this filling. Just chop it up and mix in with the rest of the ingredients in step 1.*

1. **Make the filling:** In a skillet over medium heat, cook the spinach for 1 to 2 minutes, gently stirring, until it wilts. Remove from the heat and transfer to a bowl to cool. When cool enough to handle, squeeze out as much excess water as possible. Roughly chop the spinach and set aside. In a food processor, combine the turkey, ginger, and cornstarch and pulse to form a coarse paste. Add the wilted spinach and pulse to mix.

2. Transfer the mixture to a medium bowl and stir in the black bean sauce. Cover and refrigerate while you roll the dough, or up to 1 day.

3. **Fold the dumplings:** While working, keep the wrappers covered. Lay 6 wrappers on a cutting board and place 1 tablespoon of filling in the center of each. Moisten the outer edges of the wrappers with cornstarch slurry.

4. Fold the dumplings using the Parcel Fold (see page 29). Repeat with the remaining wrappers and filling.

5. **Cook and serve:** In medium stockpot, bring 8 cups of water to a boil and add the salt. Stir to dissolve.

6. Add the dumplings, bring the water to a boil again, cook for 7 to 8 minutes, then add 1 cup of cold water. Bring the water to a boil again and cook the dumplings for 7 to 8 minutes more. Reduce the heat and simmer the dumplings for 2 minutes, or until they float. Using a spider, transfer the dumplings to a warm platter.

7. Garnish with cilantro to serve.

SPICY SHRIMP DUMPLINGS

MAKES 24 dumplings **PREP TIME** 40 minutes **COOK TIME** 25 minutes

The chili sauce in this filling gives these delicate shrimp dumplings a spicy kick. The chopped water chestnuts also add great texture to the filling. You can use Chili Crisp Sauce (page 99), but a store-bought sauce such as Lao Gan Ma works great, too.

⅔ pound shrimp, peeled, deveined, and roughly chopped

1 tablespoon cornstarch

2 teaspoons Shaoxing rice wine

1 teaspoon grated peeled fresh ginger

1 teaspoon soy sauce

¼ teaspoon kosher salt, plus 1 tablespoon

Pinch ground white pepper

¼ cup finely chopped water chestnuts

1 tablespoon Chili Crisp Sauce (page 99)

1 batch Basic Dumpling Dough (page 20), or 24 store-bought dumpling wrappers

MIX IT UP: *Use this filling with the Crystal Dumpling Dough (page 21) for a spicy twist on a classic.*

1. **Make the filling:** Set aside one-third of the chopped shrimp. In a food processor, combine the remaining chopped shrimp, cornstarch, rice wine, ginger, soy sauce, ¼ teaspoon of salt, and white pepper. Pulse to form a smooth paste.

2. Transfer the mixture to a medium bowl and stir in the reserved shrimp, water chestnuts, and chili crisp sauce. Cover and refrigerate while you roll the dough, or up to 1 day.

3. **Roll out the wrappers and fold the dumplings:** Cut the dumpling dough into 24 pieces (see page 24). Roll each piece into a 4-inch circle about ¹⁄₁₆ inch thick around the edges. Keep covered.

4. Lay 6 wrappers on a cutting board and place 1 tablespoon of filling in the center of each. If using store-bought wrappers, moisten the outer edges of the wrapper with cornstarch slurry (see page 26).

5. Fold the dumplings using the Pleated Crescent Fold (see page 27). Repeat with the remaining wrappers and filling.

6. **Cook and serve:** In medium stockpot, bring 8 cups of water to a boil and add the remaining 1 tablespoon of salt. Stir to dissolve.

7. Add the dumplings, bring the water to a boil again, and cook for 4 to 5 minutes. Reduce the heat and simmer the dumplings for 2 minutes, or until they float.

Har Gow, page 55

4

STEAMED DUMPLINGS

This chapter includes steamed dumpling classics like Shu Mai (page 50), Har Gow (page 55), and Char Siu Bao (page 54), as well as my take on popular Nepalese- and Indian-style dumplings such as momos. The famous Xiao Long Bao (page 52), also known as soup dumplings, requires a bit more effort than other recipes in this chapter, but its tasty reward far outweighs the work.

SHU MAI

MAKES 24 dumplings PREP TIME 35 minutes COOK TIME 15 minutes

Traditionally made with a pork and mushroom filling and garnished with a dab of cod roe, shu mai are small Cantonese dumplings found on dim sum menus around the world. This recipe uses minced carrot instead of fish roe to add a pop of color.

8 dried shiitake mushrooms, soaked in hot water for 15 minutes

4 ounces shrimp, peeled, deveined, and finely chopped

8 ounces ground pork

2 teaspoons cornstarch

2 tablespoons sesame oil

1 tablespoon dark soy sauce

1 tablespoon Shaoxing rice wine

1 scallion, white and green parts, minced

½ teaspoon ground white pepper

24 store-bought dumpling wrappers

Cornstarch slurry (see page 26)

¼ cup minced carrot (optional)

MAKE IT EASIER: *If you can't find round shu mai wrappers, choose square wonton wrappers and cut them into rounds with a 3½-inch round cookie cutter.*

1. **Make the filling:** Drain the mushrooms, squeezing out the excess liquid. Trim off the stems and finely mince the caps. Transfer to a medium bowl and add the shrimp, ground pork, cornstarch, sesame oil, soy sauce, rice wine, scallion, and white pepper. Stir to combine into a smooth paste.

2. **Fold the dumplings:** While working, keep the wrappers covered. Lay 6 wrappers on a cutting board and place 1 tablespoon of filling in the center of each.

3. Gather the edge of the wrapper around the filling to form an open cup shape. With your dominant hand, make a circle using the tip of your thumb and index finger (the universal "okay" sign). Hug the dumpling inside the circle formed by your thumb and index finger and shape it into a tighter cup.

4. Holding the dumpling with your thumb and index finger, lightly tap the dumpling on the work surface to flatten the bottom. The sides of the dumpling should stand straight up with an open top about 1½ inches across to expose the filling.

5. Garnish the center of the filling with minced carrot (if using). Place the dumpling into a steamer basket. Repeat the process with the remaining wrappers and filling. You should be able to fit up to 12 dumplings in a 10-inch-wide steamer basket (you'll need two baskets).

6. **Cook and serve:** In a 10-inch-wide stockpot or wok, bring 3 cups of water to a boil. Stack the steamer baskets over the pot and reduce the heat to medium to keep a low simmer.

7. Steam for 7 to 9 minutes, or until the dumpling skins look translucent and slightly wrinkly around the filling. When the dumplings are fully cooked, the internal temperature of the filling should read 165°F on an instant-read thermometer. Check and add more water to the pot, if necessary.

8. Remove the baskets from the wok and place on platters. Serve the dumplings directly from the baskets.

XIAO LONG BAO

MAKES 24 dumplings **PREP TIME** 3 hours for soup; 40 minutes for dumplings
COOK TIME 20 minutes

Your local butcher shop should have most of the ingredients for this classic soup dumpling, but try an Asian supermarket if you're having trouble finding chicken feet or pork bones. The process of making these dumplings is more involved, but the juicy dumplings at the end are so worth it!

FOR THE SOUP

8 ounces skin-on pork belly, halved

1 pound pork bones

8 ounces chicken feet

1 bunch scallions, white and green parts, roughly chopped

4-inch piece fresh ginger, peeled and thinly sliced

2 tablespoons Shaoxing rice wine

1 teaspoon kosher salt

FOR THE FILLING

⅔ pound ground pork

2 scallions, white and green parts, minced

1 garlic clove, minced

2 teaspoons sesame oil

2 teaspoons light soy sauce

1 teaspoon Shaoxing rice wine

½ teaspoon sugar

Pinch ground white pepper

1. **Make the soup:** One to two days in advance, in a medium stockpot, combine the pork belly and enough water to cover. Bring to a boil, then remove from the heat. Rinse the meat with cold water. Halve the pork belly lengthwise and separate the meat from the skin. Scrape the fat from the skin and slice the skin into ¼-inch strips. Trim the fat from the belly and cut the belly into ½-inch chunks.

2. In a stockpot, combine the cooked and sliced pork skin and belly, pork bones, chicken feet, scallions, ginger, rice wine, and 8 cups of cold water to cover. Bring to a boil over high heat, skimming off the foam occasionally. Boil for 5 minutes, then reduce the heat to medium and simmer for about 1 hour to 1 hour 30 minutes, or until the stock reduces to 2 cups. Season with salt.

3. Strain the stock into a 9-by-13-inch baking dish, discarding the solids. Let cool on the counter for 1 hour, then transfer to the refrigerator to chill completely, preferably overnight. The stock will become jelly when chilled. Keep covered until ready to use.

4. **Make the filling:** In a medium bowl, combine the ground pork, scallions, garlic, sesame oil, soy sauce, rice wine, sugar, and white pepper. Gently stir the ingredients in one direction until thoroughly combined.

**FOR THE
DUMPLINGS**

**1 batch Basic Dump-
ling Dough (page 20)**

**6 to 8 broad Napa
cabbage leaves**

**Soy-Vinegar
Dipping Sauce (page
98), for serving**

MAKE IT EASIER:
*Tackle this recipe in
stages. The soup can
keep for up to 1 week
in the refrigerator, or
up to 3 months in the
freezer. You can also
prepare the filling up
to 2 days ahead.*

5. Cut the jellied stock into ⅛-inch cubes. Scoop out one-third of the cubes into a bowl and set aside. Mix the remaining cubes into the filling. Cover and refrigerate while you roll the dough, or up to 2 days.

6. **Roll out the wrappers and fold the dumplings:** Cut the dough into 24 pieces (see page 24). Roll each piece into a 4-inch circle about 1/16 inch thick around the edges. Keep covered.

7. Lay 6 wrappers on a cutting board and place 1 tablespoon of filling in the center of each and use a spoon to flatten it slightly. Place 1 reserved cube of stock jelly on top of the filling.

8. Fold the dumplings using the Soup Dumpling Fold (see page 30). Repeat with the remaining wrappers, filling, and stock.

9. **Cook and serve:** In a 10-inch-wide stockpot or wok, bring 3 cups water to a boil. Line the bottom of two steamer baskets with the cabbage leaves and steam for 2 minutes, or until the cabbage is softened.

10. Arrange 12 dumplings in each basket, making sure they are not touching. Stack the baskets over the pot and reduce the heat to medium to keep a simmer. Steam for 10 to 12 minutes, or until the dumpling skins look dry on the surface and slightly droopy.

11. Remove from the heat and serve the dumplings directly from the baskets with the dipping sauce on the side. Be careful not to break the dumplings, or the soup will run out before you can enjoy it! Use caution when eating—the soup inside is boiling hot, so serve each dumpling in a large spoon and gently blow on it to cool before eating.

CHAR SIU BAO

MAKES 24 dumplings **PREP TIME** 40 minutes, plus 30 minutes to proof
COOK TIME 20 minutes

Char siu is a Cantonese-style barbecue pork that you can buy ready-made from the hot foods counters at Asian markets. These fluffy pork buns are a favorite in my family.

1 tablespoon sugar

1 tablespoon hoisin sauce

1 tablespoon oyster sauce

1 tablespoon cornstarch dissolved in 1 tablespoon water

2 teaspoons soy sauce

1 teaspoon Shaoxing rice wine

12 ounces char siu, cut into ¼-inch dice

1 teaspoon minced scallion, white and green parts

1 garlic clove, minced

1 batch Bao Dough (page 22)

MIX IT UP: *Don't leave this bao just for the barbecue pork! Try any of the vegetable fillings, like the one used in the Cabbage and Mushroom Gyoza (page 71), for a change.*

1. **Make the filling:** In a small saucepan over medium heat, stir together ¼ cup of water, the sugar, hoisin, oyster sauce, cornstarch mixture, soy sauce, and rice wine. Simmer for 4 to 5 minutes, or until thickened.

2. Remove from the heat and stir in the char siu, scallion, and garlic until well mixed. Let cool to room temperature, then refrigerate until the dough is rolled, or for up to 2 days.

3. **Prepare the dough and shape the baos:** Cut the dough into 24 equal pieces (see page 24). Keep the dough pieces covered under plastic wrap. Cut parchment paper into 24 (2-inch) squares.

4. Use your fingertips to flatten and stretch one piece of dough into a 4-inch circle. Place the circle flat on one palm. Spoon 1 heaping tablespoon of filling into the center. Gather the edges of the dough together and pinch tightly at the top. Place the bao, pinched-side up, on a parchment square, then place it into a stainless-steel steaming basket. Repeat with the remaining dough and filling, arranging the baos 2 inches apart in the steamer baskets.

5. **Cook and serve:** Stack the baskets, covering the top tier loosely with plastic wrap. Let rise at room temperature for 30 minutes.

6. In a 10-inch-wide stockpot or wok, bring 3 cups water to a boil. Stack the baskets over the pot and steam the baos over high heat for 12 to 15 minutes, replenishing the pot with water, as needed.

HAR GOW

MAKES 24 dumplings **PREP TIME** 40 minutes **COOK TIME** 15 minutes

These iconic steamed dumplings steal the show on any dim sum cart. Their translucent wrappers give us a peek into the mouthwatering, blush-colored shrimp filling inside. Serve these directly from the baskets with the dipping sauce on the side.

12 ounces shrimp, peeled, deveined, and roughly chopped

¼ cup minced bamboo shoots

1 tablespoon cornstarch

1 teaspoon grated peeled fresh ginger

1 teaspoon Shaoxing rice wine

1 teaspoon sesame oil

½ teaspoon soy sauce

1 batch Crystal Dumpling Dough (page 21)

Nonstick cooking spray

Soy-Vinegar Dipping Sauce (page 98), for serving

COOKING TIP: *This dumpling dough is very pliable, so you can use a tortilla press to create wrappers with a consistent thickness and size.*

1. **Make the filling:** Set ½ cup of shrimp aside. In a food processor, combine the remaining shrimp, bamboo shoots, cornstarch, ginger, rice wine, sesame oil, and soy sauce. Pulse to form a coarse paste. Transfer the mixture to a medium bowl and stir in the reserved shrimp. Cover the bowl and refrigerate for 30 minutes, or up to 1 day.

2. **Roll out the wrappers and fold the dumplings:** Cut the dough into 24 equal pieces (see page 24). Roll each piece into a 4-inch circle about 1⁄16 inch thick around the edges. Keep covered.

3. Lay 6 wrappers on a cutting board and place 1 tablespoon of filling in the center of each.

4. Fold the dumplings using the Pleated Crescent Fold (see page 27). Repeat with the remaining wrappers and filling.

5. **Cook and serve:** In a 10-inch-wide stockpot or wok, bring 3 cups water to a boil. Reduce the heat to medium to keep a simmer.

6. Lightly coat the bottoms of two steamer baskets with cooking spray. Arrange the dumplings in the baskets with at least 1 inch of space around them.

7. Stack the baskets over the pot and return the water to a boil. Reduce the heat to medium to keep a simmer. Steam for 8 to 9 minutes, or until the filling turns pink and the wrappers are translucent.

PORK AND BOK CHOY JIAOZI

MAKES 24 dumplings **PREP TIME** 45 minutes **COOK TIME** 15 minutes

The quintessential steamed pork dumplings, these jiaozi have a juicy filling with bits of salted bok choy for a crunchy texture.

2 baby bok choy bulbs, roughly chopped

2 teaspoons kosher salt

12 ounces ground pork

3 scallions, white and green parts, minced

1 tablespoon Shaoxing rice wine

2 teaspoons sesame oil

1 teaspoon cornstarch

Pinch ground white pepper

1 batch Basic Dumpling Dough (see page 20)

Nonstick cooking spray

Soy-Vinegar Dipping Sauce (page 98) or XO Sauce (page 100), for serving

MIX IT UP: *This filling can be used for wontons, potstickers, and even shengjian bao. It's the universal filling!*

1. **Make the filling:** Wilt the bok choy with the salt for 5 to 10 minutes. Squeeze out the extra moisture.

2. Transfer to a bowl and add the ground pork, scallions, rice wine, sesame oil, cornstarch, and white pepper. Mix thoroughly to combine. Cover and refrigerate while you roll the dough, or up to 2 days.

3. **Roll out the wrappers and fold the dumplings:** Cut the dough into 24 pieces (see page 24). Roll each piece into a 4-inch circle about 1/16 inch thick around the edges. Keep covered.

4. Lay 6 wrappers on a cutting board and place 1 tablespoon of filling in the center of each.

5. Fold using the Pleated Crescent Fold (see page 27). Repeat with the remaining wrappers and filling.

6. **Cook and serve:** In a 10-inch-wide stockpot or wok, bring 3 cups water to a boil. Reduce the heat to medium to keep a simmer.

7. Lightly coat the bottoms of two steamer baskets with cooking spray. Arrange the dumplings in the steamer baskets without letting them touch.

8. Stack the baskets over the pot and return the water to a boil. Reduce the heat to medium to keep a simmer. Steam for 8 to 9 minutes, adding more water, as needed.

9. Remove the baskets from the pot and serve the dumplings directly from the baskets with the dipping sauce on the side.

CHICKEN MOMOS WITH TOMATO SESAME CHUTNEY

MAKES 24 dumplings **PREP TIME** 1 hour **COOK TIME** 20 minutes

These flavorful dumplings are inspired by Tibetan momos, which are traditionally served with a deliciously spicy tomato sauce. To morph this into a hearty soup, stir about 3 cups hot chicken stock into the sauce.

FOR THE CHUTNEY

1 tablespoon unsalted butter

3 garlic cloves, smashed

1-inch piece fresh ginger, peeled and chopped

1 tablespoon curry powder

1 (15-ounce) can crushed fire-roasted tomatoes

Pinch kosher salt

1 cup chopped fresh cilantro

1 tablespoon sesame oil

1 tablespoon freshly squeezed lemon juice

FOR THE CHICKEN MOMOS

1 cup shredded Napa cabbage

1½ teaspoons kosher salt, divided

12 ounces ground chicken

1 shallot, roughly chopped

1. **Make the chutney:** In a saucepan over medium heat, melt the butter. Add the garlic, ginger, and curry powder and sauté for 25 to 30 seconds. Stir in the tomatoes and simmer for 15 minutes.

2. Remove from the heat and let cool slightly. Season with salt, then blend the chutney using an immersion blender, or transfer to a standard blender and blend until smooth. Stir in the cilantro, sesame oil, and lemon juice. Set aside.

3. **Make the filling:** In a wire-mesh strainer, toss the cabbage with 1 teaspoon of salt and let sit over a bowl for 10 minutes, or until the cabbage has wilted. Squeeze out the excess moisture from the cabbage (no need to rinse it first).

4. In a food processor, combine the cabbage, ground chicken, shallot, garlic, ginger, curry powder, and remaining ½ teaspoon of salt. Pulse to form a smooth paste.

5. **Fold the dumplings:** While working, keep the wrappers covered. Lay 6 wrappers on a cutting board and place 1 tablespoon of filling in the center of each. Moisten the outer edges of the wrapper with cornstarch slurry.

6. Fold the dumplings using the Pleated Crescent Fold (see page 27). Repeat with the remaining wrappers and filling.

continues ▶

3 garlic cloves, smashed

½-inch piece fresh ginger, peeled and coarsely chopped

1 teaspoon curry powder

24 store-bought dumpling wrappers

Cornstarch slurry (see page 26)

Nonstick cooking spray

COOKING TIP: *A delicious substitute for the chicken is ground turkey.*

7. **Cook and serve:** In a 10-inch-wide stockpot or wok, bring 3 cups water to a boil. Reduce the heat to medium to keep a simmer.

8. Lightly coat the bottoms of two steamer baskets with cooking spray. Arrange the dumplings in the steamer baskets, with at least 1 inch of space around them.

9. Stack the baskets over the pot and return the water to a boil. Reduce the heat to medium to keep a simmer. Steam for 10 to 12 minutes, adding more water, as needed.

10. Remove the baskets from the heat and let rest for 2 minutes. Divide the tomato chutney among shallow bowls and equally distribute the dumplings.

PANEER MOMO JHOL IN SPICY TOMATO SOUP

MAKES 24 dumplings **PREP TIME** 1 hour **COOK TIME** 15 minutes

Popular in Nepal, jhol momos are traditionally made with meat fillings and served with a tomato-based chutney or soup.

2 tablespoons
unsalted butter

1 medium onion,
grated, divided

4 garlic cloves, minced

1-inch piece fresh ginger,
peeled and minced, divided

Pinch kosher salt

1 tablespoon curry powder

3 teaspoons Chinese
five-spice powder, divided

3 cups vegetable stock

1 (15-ounce) can fire-roasted
crushed tomatoes

1 (10-ounce) package
frozen spinach, defrosted,
squeezed, and chopped

1½ cups grated paneer
or queso fresco (about
6 ounces)

1 batch Basic Dumpling
Dough (page 20)

Nonstick cooking spray

MAKE IT EASIER: *Save some
time by using store-bought
wonton wrappers.*

1. **Make the soup:** In a large saucepan over medium-high heat, melt the butter. Add half the onion, the garlic, and half the ginger. Sauté for 2 minutes, or until the onion is soft and translucent. Season with salt, curry powder, and 2 teaspoons of five-spice powder.

2. In a blender, combine the cooked vegetables, vegetable stock, and tomatoes. Blend until smooth. Transfer the mixture to the saucepan and simmer for 20 minutes. Keep warm while you prepare the dumplings.

3. **Make the filling:** In a medium bowl, combine the spinach, paneer, remaining onion, remaining ginger, and the remaining 1 teaspoon of five-spice powder and stir until combined.

4. **Roll out the wrappers and fold the dumplings:** Cut the dough into 24 pieces (see page 24). Roll each piece into a 4-inch circle about 1/16 inch thick around the edges. Keep covered.

5. Lay 6 wrappers on a cutting board and place 1 tablespoon of filling in the center of each.

6. Fold the dumplings using the Soup Dumpling Fold (see page 30). Repeat with the remaining wrappers and filling.

7. **Cook and serve:** In a 10-inch-wide stockpot or wok, bring 3 cups water to a boil. Reduce the heat to medium to keep a simmer.

VEGETARIAN

continues ▶

8. Lightly coat the bottoms of two steamer baskets with cooking spray. Place the dumplings in the steamer baskets, careful not to crowd them.

9. Stack the baskets over the pot and return the water to a boil. Reduce the heat to medium to keep a simmer. Steam for 8 to 10 minutes, adding more water, as needed.

10. Remove from heat and let rest for 2 minutes before serving.

EGGPLANT AND WATER CHESTNUT HALF-MOONS

MAKES 24 dumplings **PREP TIME** 40 minutes **COOK TIME** 20 minutes

The humble eggplant can transform into a fantastic dumpling filling with the help of the umami-rich black bean sauce. This recipe calls for water chestnuts for some crunch, but you can use bamboo shoots or celery instead.

2 tablespoons vegetable oil

1 medium eggplant, cut into ¼-inch cubes

Pinch kosher salt

½ medium onion, finely chopped

1 (4-ounce) can water chestnuts, drained and roughly chopped

¼ cup black bean sauce

2 scallions, white and green parts, minced

1 batch Basic Dumpling Dough (page 20)

Nonstick cooking spray

MIX IT UP: *Make a spicier dumpling by adding 2 teaspoons Chili Crisp Sauce (page 99) to the filling.*

1. **Make the filling:** In a skillet over medium-high heat, heat the vegetable oil. Swirl to coat the skillet and add the eggplant. Sauté for 1 minute, then add the salt and onion. Cook for 5 to 7 minutes, or until the eggplant becomes golden.

2. Stir in the water chestnuts and black bean sauce. Remove from the heat and let cool. Stir in the scallions and transfer the filling to a medium bowl to cool.

3. **Roll out the wrappers and fold the dumplings:** Cut the dough into 24 pieces (see page 24). Roll each piece into a 4-inch circle about ¹⁄₁₆ inch thick around the edges. Keep covered.

4. Lay 6 wrappers on a cutting board and place 1 tablespoon of filling in the center of each.

5. Fold the dumplings using the Basic Half-Moon Fold (see page 26). Repeat with the remaining wrappers and filling.

6. **Cook and serve:** In a 10-inch-wide stockpot or wok, bring 4 cups water to a boil. Reduce the heat to medium to keep a simmer.

7. Lightly coat the bottoms of two steamer baskets with cooking spray. Arrange the dumplings in the steamer baskets, leaving at least 1 inch of space between each.

VEGAN

continues ▶

8. Stack the baskets over the pot and return the water to a boil. Reduce the heat to medium to keep a simmer. Steam for 8 to 10 minutes, adding more water, as needed.

9. Remove the baskets from the wok and serve the dumplings directly from the baskets.

CRYSTAL CHIVE DUMPLINGS

MAKES 24 dumplings **PREP TIME** 40 minutes **COOK TIME** 15 minutes

These are traditionally made with shrimp filling, but here's a vegan-friendly version. If you can't find Chinese garlic chives, use regular chives or scallions.

2 tablespoons vegetable oil

4 ounces fresh shiitake mushrooms, stemmed and roughly chopped

Pinch kosher salt

1 (10-ounce) package frozen spinach, defrosted, squeezed, and chopped

½ bunch fresh Chinese garlic chives, roughly chopped

2 garlic cloves, minced

1 tablespoon light soy sauce

2 teaspoons sesame oil

1 batch Crystal Dumpling Dough (page 21), at room temperature

Nonstick cooking spray

MIX IT UP: *During early spring, look for fresh pea shoots at Asian markets. They make a tasty alternative to the chives in this filling.*

1. **Make the filling:** In a skillet over medium-high heat, heat the vegetable oil. Swirl to coat the skillet and add the mushrooms. Sauté for 1 minute, then add the salt, spinach, chives, and garlic. Cook for about 2 minutes until the spinach and chives are heated through. Stir in the soy sauce and sesame oil and transfer the filling to a medium bowl to cool.

2. **Roll out the wrappers and fold the dumplings:** Cut the dough into 24 equal pieces (see page 24). Roll each piece into a 4-inch circle about 1/16 inch thick around the edges. Keep covered.

3. Lay 6 wrappers on a cutting board and place 1 tablespoon of filling in the center of each.

4. Fold the dumplings using the Basic Half-Moon Fold (see page 26). Repeat with the remaining wrappers and filling.

5. **Cook and serve:** In a 10-inch-wide stockpot or wok, bring 3 cups water to a boil. Reduce the heat to medium to keep a simmer. Lightly coat the bottoms of two steamer baskets with cooking spray. Place the dumplings in the steamer baskets, leaving at least 1 inch of space between each.

6. Stack the baskets over the pot and return the water to a boil. Reduce the heat to medium to keep a simmer. Steam for 8 to 10 minutes, adding more water, as needed.

7. Remove the baskets from the heat and serve the dumplings directly from the baskets.

VEGAN

CRYSTAL WOOD EAR AND BAMBOO SHOOT DUMPLINGS

MAKES 24 dumplings **PREP TIME** 40 minutes **COOK TIME** 20 minutes

Wood ear mushrooms lend chewiness to this filling, and the bamboo shoots add a nice crunch against the soft crystal dumpling skins. This uses a vegetarian stir-fry sauce made of shiitake mushrooms instead of the traditional oyster sauce.

VEGAN

8 ounces baked tofu

1 carrot, halved

1 (4-ounce) can sliced bamboo shoots, drained

2 tablespoons vegetable oil

1 cup roughly chopped wood ear mushrooms or any other wild mushroom

2 teaspoons grated peeled fresh ginger

2 tablespoons vegetarian stir-fry sauce

Pinch ground white pepper

1 batch Crystal Dumpling Dough (page 21)

Nonstick cooking spray

MIX IT UP: *This filling is excellent inside a potsticker or wonton, too.*

1. **Make the filling:** In a food processor, combine the tofu, carrot, and bamboo shoots. Pulse until finely chopped.

2. In a skillet over medium-high heat, heat the vegetable oil. Swirl to coat the skillet and add the tofu mixture, mushrooms, and ginger. Sauté for 3 to 4 minutes to cook off any moisture. Stir in the stir-fry sauce and white pepper and transfer the filling to a medium bowl to cool.

3. **Roll out the wrappers and fold the dumplings:** Cut the dough into 24 equal pieces (see page 24). Roll each piece into a 4-inch circle about $\frac{1}{16}$ inch thick around the edges. Keep covered.

4. Lay 6 wrappers on a cutting board and place 1 tablespoon of filling in the center of each.

5. Fold the dumplings using the Pleated Crescent Fold (see page 27). Repeat with the remaining wrappers and filling.

6. **Cook and serve:** In a 10-inch-wide stockpot or wok, bring 3 cups water to a boil. Reduce the heat to medium to keep a simmer.

7. Lightly coat the bottoms of two steamer baskets with cooking spray. Place the dumplings in the steamer baskets, being careful not to crowd them.

8. Stack the baskets over the pot and return the water to a boil. Reduce the heat to medium to keep a simmer. Steam for 8 to 10 minutes, adding more water as, needed.

9. Remove the baskets from heat and serve the dumplings directly from the baskets.

RED BEAN PASTE BAOS

MAKES 24 baos **PREP TIME** 30 minutes, plus 30 minutes to proof
COOK TIME 30 minutes

Sweetened red bean paste is a common ingredient in many Chinese desserts. The red adzuki beans are cooked in a sugar syrup, then mashed into a paste. To enhance the unique flavor of the beans, this recipe calls for a little orange zest, but this is optional.

2 (7-ounce) cans sweet red bean paste

Grated zest of 1 orange (optional)

1 batch Bao Dough (page 22)

MIX IT UP: *After steaming, pan-fry the bottoms of the baos using the potsticker cooking method (see page 70) to create a crispy-bottomed bao.*

1. **Make the filling:** In a small bowl, stir together the bean paste and orange zest (if using) until thoroughly combined. Cut 24 (2-inch) squares of parchment paper and set aside.

2. **Roll out the wrappers and fold the dumplings:** Cut the dough into 24 equal pieces (see page 24). Keep the dough pieces covered under plastic wrap.

3. Use your fingertips to flatten and stretch one piece of dough into a 3-inch circle. Place the circle flat on one palm. Spoon 1 heaping tablespoon of filling into the center. Gather the edges of the dough together and pinch tightly at the top. Place the bao, pinched-side up, on a parchment square, then place it into a stainless-steel steaming basket. Repeat with the remaining dough and filling, arranging the baos 2 inches apart in the steamer baskets, or about 6 baos per steamer basket.

4. **Cook and serve:** Stack the baskets, covering the top tier loosely with plastic wrap. Let the baos rise at room temperature for 30 minutes.

5. In a stockpot, bring 3 cups water to a boil. Stack two steamer baskets over the stockpot and steam for 12 minutes over high heat, adding more water, as needed. Repeat with the remaining baos, adding more water to the pot, as needed. Transfer the baos to a warm platter.

VEGAN

Classic Pork Potstickers, page 70

5

PAN-FRIED AND FRIED DUMPLINGS

These dumplings are popular for their crispy, crunchy texture. Pan-fried dumplings are first steamed, then lightly fried with a small amount of oil to create a golden-brown crust. Deep-fried dumplings don't require steaming and yield extra crispy wrappers with a tender filling inside. Here, you'll find classics like potstickers and fried wontons, as well as some creative takes on traditional flavors.

CLASSIC PORK POTSTICKERS

MAKES 24 dumplings **PREP TIME** 1 hour **COOK TIME** 30 minutes

My mom always kept a bag of homemade potstickers in the freezer. My brother would cook up a batch for an after-school snack. It was the most satisfying treat ever.

2 cups finely shredded Napa cabbage

1 tablespoon kosher salt

²/₃ pound ground pork

½-inch piece fresh ginger, peeled and minced

1 tablespoon light soy sauce

1 tablespoon sesame oil

2 teaspoons Shaoxing rice wine

1 batch Basic Dumpling dough (page 20)

2 tablespoons vegetable oil, divided

MIX IT UP: *Try this method with the filling from the Spicy Shrimp Dumplings (page 47) and let me know what you think!*

1. **Make the filling:** Wilt the cabbage with the salt and let sit for 30 minutes, or until the cabbage has wilted. Rinse, then squeeze out as much water as possible.

2. In a medium bowl, toss together the cabbage, ground pork, ginger, soy sauce, sesame oil, and rice wine until combined. Refrigerate while you roll the dough, or up to 2 hours.

3. **Roll out the wrappers and fold the dumplings:** Cut the dough into 24 equal pieces (see page 24). Roll each piece into a 4-inch circle about ¹/₁₆ inch thick around the edges. Keep covered.

4. Lay 6 wrappers on a cutting board and place 1 tablespoon of filling in the center of each wrapper.

5. Fold using the Pleated Crescent Fold (see page 27). Repeat with the remaining wrappers and filling.

6. **Cook and serve:** In a large nonstick skillet over medium-high heat, heat 1 tablespoon of vegetable oil. When the oil is almost smoking, arrange half the potstickers in the skillet without letting them touch. Pan-fry for 2 to 3 minutes.

7. Carefully pour ²/₃ cup water into the skillet and cover the pan. Once the water comes to a boil, reduce the heat to low and simmer for 6 to 7 minutes.

8. Uncover and increase the heat to medium-high. Cook for 2 to 3 minutes, or until all the water has evaporated and the potsticker bottoms are browned and crisp. Repeat with the remaining dumplings and oil.

CABBAGE AND MUSHROOM GYOZA

MAKES 24 dumplings **PREP TIME** 1 hour **COOK TIME** 30 minutes

Japanese gyoza are usually made with thinner wrappers than Chinese potstickers. They are less chewy, and the bottoms are crispier. Make another batch to freeze and have on hand whenever the craving strikes!

2 cups finely shredded green cabbage

1 tablespoon kosher salt

4 dried shiitake mushrooms

8 large fresh shiitake mushrooms, stemmed and finely chopped

½-inch piece fresh ginger, peeled and minced

1 tablespoon soy sauce or tamari

1 teaspoon rice vinegar

24 store-bought gyoza wrappers

Cornstarch slurry (see page 26)

2 tablespoons vegetable oil, divided

MIX IT UP: *Pork and cabbage is a classic gyoza filling.*

1. **Make the filling:** Wilt the cabbage with the salt and let sit for 30 minutes. Rinse, then squeeze out as much water as possible.

2. In a food processor, pulse the dried shiitake mushrooms until nearly powdered. Add the fresh mushrooms, cabbage, ginger, soy sauce, and rice wine and pulse until thoroughly combined. Cover and set aside.

3. **Fold the dumplings:** Lay 6 wrappers on a cutting board and place 1 tablespoon of filling in the center of each. Moisten the outer edges of the wrapper with cornstarch slurry.

4. Fold using the Pleated Crescent Fold (see page 27). Repeat with the remaining wrappers and filling.

5. **Cook and serve:** In a large nonstick skillet over medium-high heat, heat 1 tablespoon of vegetable oil and swirl to coat the skillet. When the oil is almost smoking, arrange half the gyoza in the skillet without letting them touch. Pan-fry for 2 to 3 minutes. Reduce the heat if the gyoza are browning too quickly.

6. Carefully pour ⅔ cup water into the skillet and cover the pan. Once the water comes to a boil, reduce the heat to low and simmer for 6 to 7 minutes.

7. Remove the lid and increase the heat to medium-high. Cook for 2 to 3 minutes, or until all the water has evaporated and the gyoza bottoms are browned and crisp. Repeat with the remaining dumplings.

VEGAN

KIMCHI MANDU

MAKES 24 dumplings **PREP TIME** 45 minutes **COOK TIME** 30 minutes

Kimchi is briny, crunchy, and so delicious. If you're like me, you've probably got a jar in the back of your refrigerator, and this dumpling is a great way to use it up. And an accompaniment to these dumplings? More kimchi, of course!

2 cups mung bean sprouts

1 tablespoon kosher salt

1½ cups kimchi

8 ounces firm tofu, diced

1 small shallot, roughly chopped

3 scallions, white and green parts, roughly chopped

2 garlic cloves, roughly chopped

1 large egg

1 teaspoon sesame oil

1 batch Basic Dumpling Dough (page 20)

2 tablespoons vegetable oil, divided

MIX IT UP: *These dumplings work well steamed or in a soup, like Hot and Sour Soup (page 93).*

1. **Make the filling:** In a saucepan, bring 4 cups water to a boil. Add the bean sprouts and salt. Return the water to a boil, drain, and rinse the sprouts under cold water. Set aside to drain well.

2. In a food processor, combine the kimchi, tofu, shallot, scallions, and garlic and pulse until finely chopped. Squeeze out excess water from the sprouts and add them to the processor. Add the egg and sesame oil and pulse to combine.

3. Transfer the mixture to a medium bowl and refrigerate while you roll the dough, or up to 2 days.

4. **Roll out the wrappers and fold the dumplings:** Cut the dough into 24 equal pieces (see page 24). Roll each piece into a 4-inch circle about 1/16 inch thick around the edges. Keep covered.

5. Lay 6 wrappers on a cutting board and place 1 tablespoon of filling in the center of each.

6. Fold the dumplings using the Pleated Crescent Fold (see page 27). Repeat with the remaining wrappers and filling.

7. **Cook and serve:** In a large nonstick skillet over medium-high heat, heat 1 tablespoon of vegetable oil and swirl to coat the skillet. When the oil is almost smoking, arrange half the dumplings in the skillet without letting them touch. Pan-fry for 2 to 3 minutes. Reduce the heat if browning too quickly.

VEGETARIAN

8. Carefully pour 1/2 cup water into the skillet and cover the pan. Once the water comes to a boil, reduce the heat to low and simmer for 6 to 7 minutes.

9. Remove the lid and increase the heat to medium-high. Cook for 2 to 3 minutes, or until all the water has evaporated and the mandu bottoms are browned and crisp. Repeat with the remaining dumplings and oil.

PAN-FRIED CHICKEN AND GREEN BEAN MOMOS

MAKES 24 dumplings **PREP TIME** 35 minutes **COOK TIME** 30 minutes

The chewy-crunchy texture of this dumpling skin works well with its chicken filling studded with crunchy bits of green bean. Momos and dumplings are virtually the same thing— steamed dumplings with a flour-based wrapper.

²/₃ pound ground chicken (dark meat preferred)

2 tablespoons cornstarch

1 tablespoon oyster sauce

2 teaspoons sesame oil

½-inch piece fresh ginger, peeled and minced

1 cup green beans, cut into ¼-inch pieces

1 batch Basic Dumpling Dough (page 20)

2 tablespoons vegetable oil, divided

MIX IT UP: *For a deeper umami flavor, use black bean sauce instead of oyster sauce. For a sweeter flavor, try hoisin sauce.*

1. **Make the filling:** In a medium bowl, stir together the ground chicken, cornstarch, oyster sauce, sesame oil, and ginger until smooth. Fold in the green beans, cover the bowl, and refrigerate while you roll the dough, or up to 2 days.

2. **Roll out the wrappers and fold the dumplings:** Cut the dough into 24 equal pieces (see page 24). Roll each piece into a 4-inch circle about ¹/₁₆ inch thick around the edges. Keep covered.

3. Lay 6 wrappers on a cutting board and place 1 tablespoon of filling in the center of each.

4. Fold the dumplings using the Soup Dumpling Fold (see page 30). Repeat with the remaining wrappers and filling.

5. **Cook and serve:** In a large nonstick skillet over medium-high heat, heat 1 tablespoon of vegetable oil and swirl to coat the skillet. When the oil is almost smoking, pan-fry half the dumplings in the skillet for 2 to 3 minutes.

6. Carefully pour ¼ cup water into the skillet and cover the pan. Once the water comes to a boil, reduce the heat to low and simmer for 6 to 7 minutes.

7. Uncover and increase the heat to medium-high. Cook for 2 to 3 minutes, or until all the water has evaporated and the momo bottoms are browned and crisp. Repeat with the remaining batch.

SHENGJIAN BAO (PAN-FRIED PORK BUNS)

MAKES 24 dumplings **PREP TIME** 35 minutes, plus 30 minutes to proof
COOK TIME 30 minutes

Traditionally served as a breakfast item, these classic Shanghainese-style pork buns are fluffy on the outside and filled with savory pork on the inside. They are a favorite of our family for weekend brunch.

2/3 pound ground pork

2 scallions, white and green parts, minced

1 tablespoon light soy sauce

1 teaspoon grated peeled fresh ginger

1 teaspoon Shaoxing rice wine

1 teaspoon sesame oil

Pinch Chinese five-spice powder

1/3 cup chicken stock

1 batch Bao Dough (page 22)

2 tablespoons vegetable oil

1 tablespoon sesame seeds, toasted

MAKE IT EASIER: *Mix the filling in a stand mixer with a paddle attachment on medium speed for 1 minute.*

1. **Make the filling:** In a large bowl, stir together the ground pork, scallions, soy sauce, ginger, rice wine, sesame oil, and five-spice powder until combined and smooth.

2. Add the chicken stock, 2 tablespoons at a time, and stir until mixed in completely. Cover and refrigerator while you roll the dough, or up to 1 day.

3. **Prepare the dough and shape the baos:** Cut the dough into 24 equal pieces (see page 24). Keep covered.

4. Line a baking sheet with parchment paper.

5. Use your fingertips to flatten and stretch one piece of dough into a 4-inch circle. Place the circle flat on one palm. Spoon 1 heaping tablespoon of filling into the center. Gather the edges of the dough together and pinch tightly at the top to seal the edges. Place the bao, pinched-side up, on the prepared baking sheet, leaving about 2 inches between each bao. Repeat with the remaining dough and filling.

6. Loosely cover the buns and let rise for 20 to 30 minutes, or until they feel puffy.

continues ▶

7. **Cook and serve:** In a large nonstick skillet over medium-high heat, heat 1 tablespoon of vegetable oil until shimmering. Arrange half the buns in the pan, leaving ½ inch of space between each bun. Pan-fry for 30 seconds, or until the bun bottoms are pale-golden brown.

8. Pour ¼ cup water into the skillet and cover the pan immediately. Cook for 8 to 10 minutes, or until the water evaporates completely.

9. Turn off the heat and leave the lid on for 1 minute, or until the sizzling stops. The baos should have bottoms that are golden brown and crispy. Transfer to a warm plate and repeat with the remaining buns.

10. Sprinkle with sesame seeds to serve.

DEEP-FRIED TURKEY WONTONS

MAKES 24 wontons **PREP TIME** 35 minutes **COOK TIME** 30 minutes

I love using ground turkey for deep-fried wontons instead of pork when I want a lighter filling. Using dried mushrooms keeps the filling from becoming too wet, which would explode in the hot oil.

4 dried shiitake mushrooms

8 ounces ground turkey (dark meat preferred)

2 tablespoons minced peeled fresh ginger

1 tablespoon mushroom soy sauce or light soy sauce

1 tablespoon sesame oil

2 teaspoons Shaoxing rice wine

Pinch ground white pepper

24 store-bought wonton wrappers

Cornstarch slurry (see page 26)

3 cups canola oil

Generous pinch kosher salt

COOKING TIP: *I prefer using ground turkey for deep-fried wontons instead of pork because it's leaner, which makes a dumpling that's not so heavy; however, use ground dark meat turkey, so the filling doesn't turn out dry.*

1. **Make the filling:** In a food processor, process the mushrooms until finely ground. Add the ground turkey, ginger, soy sauce, sesame oil, rice wine, and white pepper. Pulse to combine, then process to form a smooth paste. Transfer the filling to a medium bowl.

2. **Fold the dumplings:** While working, keep the wrappers covered. Lay 6 wrappers on a cutting board and place 1 tablespoon of filling in the center of each. Moisten the outer edges of the wrappers with cornstarch slurry.

3. Fold the dumplings using the Classic Wonton Fold (see page 28). Repeat with the remaining wrappers and filling.

4. **Cook and serve:** In a wok or Dutch oven over medium-high heat, heat the canola oil to 375°F. Set a wire rack over a sheet pan and set aside.

5. Working in batches of 4 to 6 wontons, gently lower the wontons into the hot oil. Use a skimmer to flip the wontons or to keep them submerged in the hot oil. Fry for 5 to 6 minutes, or until browned and crispy.

6. Using a skimmer, transfer the wontons from the hot oil to the prepared wire rack. Sprinkle with salt while still hot.

CRAB RANGOONS

MAKES 24 dumplings **PREP TIME** 35 minutes **COOK TIME** 30 minutes

"Have you ever had these before? They are little bites of heaven!" is how my friend Shannon introduced me to these delicious deep-fried crab puffs. Crab rangoons were first developed in San Francisco as an appetizer; but really, any time is a good time for these crispy delights!

4 ounces fresh crabmeat, cartilage removed, picked through, and squeezed of extra moisture

8 ounces cream cheese, at room temperature

1 scallion, white and green parts, minced

1 teaspoon Worcestershire sauce

¼ teaspoon garlic powder

Pinch kosher salt, plus more for seasoning

Pinch ground white pepper

24 store-bought wonton wrappers

Cornstarch slurry (see page 26)

3 cups canola oil

COOKING TIP: *Canned crab or imitation crab sticks (also called surimi or seafood cocktail sticks) also work well here and would be cheaper than crab.*

1. **Make the filling:** Set aside 2 tablespoons of crabmeat. In a medium bowl, combine the remaining crab, cream cheese, scallion, Worcestershire sauce, garlic powder, salt, and white pepper. Mix thoroughly until smooth and fold in the reserved crab.

2. **Fold the dumplings:** While working, keep the wrappers covered.

3. Lay 6 wrappers on a cutting board and place 1 tablespoon of filling in the center of each. Moisten the outer edges of the wrapper with cornstarch slurry.

4. Fold the dumplings using the Parcel Fold (see page 29). Repeat with the remaining wrappers and filling.

5. **Cook and serve:** In a wok or Dutch oven over medium-high heat, heat the canola oil to 375°F. Set a wire rack over a sheet pan and set aside.

6. Working in batches of 4 to 6 dumplings at a time, gently lower the dumplings into the hot oil. Use a skimmer to flip the rangoons or to keep them submerged in the hot oil. Fry for 4 to 5 minutes, or until browned and crispy.

7. Using a skimmer, transfer the rangoons from the hot oil to the prepared rack. Sprinkle with salt while still hot.

BOK CHOY AND SALTED MUSTARD GREENS POTSTICKERS

MAKES 24 dumplings **PREP TIME** 45 minutes **COOK TIME** 30 minutes

This light and flavorful dumpling uses salted mustard greens for a briny crunch. Look for them in prepared pouches near the fresh dumpling wrappers at Asian markets.

3 tablespoons vegetable oil, divided

4 ounces baby bok choy, roughly chopped

1 small onion, grated

1 small carrot, grated

2 teaspoons grated peeled fresh ginger

Pinch kosher salt

½ cup salted mustard greens, drained and chopped

1 tablespoon vegetarian stir-fry sauce

2 teaspoons sesame oil

1 tablespoon cornstarch

1 batch Basic Dumpling Dough (page 20)

2 tablespoons vegetable oil, divided

MIX IT UP: *This bright-green filling is excellent with Crystal Dumpling Dough (page 21) wrappers, too! Pan-fry them the same way for a chewy-crispy texture with beautiful vegetables showing through.*

1. **Make the filling:** In a large skillet over medium-high heat, heat 1 tablespoon of vegetable oil, swirling to coat the skillet. When the oil just begins to smoke, add the bok choy, onion, carrot, and ginger. Season with salt and sauté for 7 to 10 minutes until the vegetables cook down.

2. Add the mustard greens, stir-fry sauce, and sesame oil and sprinkle in the cornstarch. Stir to combine. Remove from the heat and let cool while you roll the dough.

3. **Roll out the wrappers and fold the dumplings:** Cut the dough into 24 equal pieces (see page 24). Roll each piece into a 4-inch circle about ¹⁄₁₆ inch thick around the edges. Keep covered.

4. Lay 6 wrappers on a cutting board and place 1 tablespoon of filling in the center of each.

5. Fold the dumplings using the Pleated Crescent Fold (see page 27). Repeat with the remaining wrappers and filling.

6. **Cook and serve:** In a large nonstick skillet over medium-high heat, heat 1 tablespoon of vegetable oil, swirling to coat the skillet. When the oil is almost smoking, arrange half the potstickers in the skillet as close to one another as possible without letting them touch. Pan-fry for 2 to 3 minutes, or until golden brown.

VEGAN

continues ▶

7. Carefully pour ½ cup water into the skillet and cover the pan. Once the water boils, reduce the heat to low and simmer for 6 to 7 minutes.

8. Uncover and increase the heat to medium-high. Cook for 2 to 3 minutes, or until all the water has evaporated and the bottoms of the potstickers are browned. Repeat with the remaining potstickers and oil. Serve browned-side up.

PORK AND CHICKEN MANDU

MAKES 24 dumplings **PREP TIME** 35 minutes **COOK TIME** 30 minutes

Mandu are prepared for Lunar New Year celebrations throughout Korea. They can be boiled, steamed, or pan-fried. This recipe calls for blended pork and chicken for the filling, but feel free to experiment with any combinations you like.

⅓ pound ground pork

⅓ pound ground chicken

Generous pinch kosher salt

¼ head green cabbage, grated

1 cup roughly chopped mung bean sprouts

1 small onion, grated

2 tablespoons soy sauce

1 tablespoon sesame oil

3 garlic cloves, minced

1 batch Basic Dumpling Dough (see page 20)

2 tablespoons vegetable oil, divided

Soy-Vinegar Dipping Sauce (page 98), for serving

MIX IT UP: *Turn your gun mandu (pan-fried dumplings) into jjin mandu (steamed dumplings) by following the cooking directions for other steamed dumplings in chapter 4.*

1. **Make the filling:** In a large bowl, stir together the ground pork, ground chicken, and salt. Mix thoroughly until the proteins are combined into a smooth paste. Add the cabbage, bean sprouts, onion, soy sauce, sesame oil, and garlic and continue to mix the ingredients until combined. Cover and refrigerate while you roll the dough, or up to 2 days.

2. **Roll out the wrappers and fold the dumplings:** Cut the dough into 24 equal pieces (see page 24). Roll each piece into a 4-inch circle about ¹⁄₁₆ inch thick around the edges. Keep covered.

3. Lay 6 wrappers on a cutting board and place 1 tablespoon of filling in the center of each.

4. Fold using the Classic Wonton Fold (see page 28). Repeat with the remaining wrappers and filling.

5. **Cook and serve:** In a large nonstick skillet over medium-high heat, heat 1 tablespoon of vegetable oil. When the oil is almost smoking, arrange half the dumplings in the skillet. Pan-fry for 2 to 3 minutes, or until golden brown.

6. Carefully pour ½ cup water into the skillet and cover the pan. Once the water boils, reduce the heat to low and simmer for 6 to 7 minutes.

7. Uncover and increase the heat to medium-high. Cook for 2 to 3 minutes, or until all the water has evaporated and the bottoms are browned. Repeat with the remaining dumplings. Serve, browned-side up, with the dipping sauce on the side.

TURKEY AND NAPA CABBAGE POTSTICKERS

MAKES 24 dumplings **PREP TIME** 1 hour 5 minutes **COOK TIME** 30 minutes

A few years ago, I had the honor of creating recipes for a dear friend's dumpling party and gave a dumpling-making lesson to his friends and family. This recipe is inspired by that party.

¼ head Napa cabbage, finely shredded

1 tablespoon kosher salt

8 ounces ground turkey

½-inch piece fresh ginger, peeled and grated

1 tablespoon hoisin sauce

2 teaspoons Shaoxing rice wine

1 tablespoon cornstarch

1 tablespoon sesame oil

1 batch Basic Dumpling Dough (see page 20)

2 tablespoons vegetable oil, divided

MIX IT UP: *This filling makes an excellent wonton filling for either Traditional Soup Wontons (see page 37) or Deep-fried Turkey Wontons (see page 77).*

1. **Make the filling:** In a wire-mesh strainer set over a bowl, toss the cabbage with the salt and let sit for 30 minutes, or until the cabbage has wilted. Rinse, then squeeze out as much water as possible.

2. In a food processor, pulse the ground turkey and ginger until well mixed. Add the hoisin, rice wine, cornstarch, and sesame oil and pulse to form a smooth paste. Add the cabbage and pulse to combine. Transfer the filling to a medium bowl, cover, and refrigerate while you roll the dough, or up to 2 hours.

3. **Roll out the wrappers and fold the dumplings:** Cut the dough into 24 equal pieces (see page 24). Roll each piece into a 4-inch circle about ¹⁄₁₆ inch thick around the edges. Keep covered.

4. Lay 6 wrappers on a cutting board and place 1 tablespoon of filling in the center of each.

5. Fold the dumplings using the Pleated Crescent Fold (see page 27). Repeat with the remaining wrappers and filling.

6. **Cook and serve:** In a large nonstick skillet over medium-high heat, heat 1 tablespoon of vegetable oil, swirling to coat the skillet. When the oil is almost smoking, arrange half the potstickers in the skillet without letting them touch. Pan-fry for 2 to 3 minutes, or until golden brown.

7. Carefully pour ⅔ cup water into the skillet and cover the pan. Once the water boils, reduce the heat to low and simmer for 6 to 7 minutes.

8. Remove the lid and increase the heat to medium-high. Cook the potstickers for 2 to 3 minutes, or until browned and crisp. Repeat with the remaining dumplings and oil.

CURRIED POTATO DUMPLINGS

MAKES 24 dumplings **PREP TIME** 50 minutes **COOK TIME** 25 minutes

These fried potato dumplings are similar to Indian samosas. The combination of potatoes and curry makes this a satisfying appetizer or snack.

1 medium russet potato, peeled and cut into ½-inch cubes

2 tablespoons kosher salt, divided

1 tablespoon unsalted butter or coconut oil

1 small shallot, minced

2 garlic cloves, minced

½-inch piece fresh ginger, peeled and grated

1 tablespoon curry powder

½ cup frozen peas, thawed

2 tablespoons roughly chopped fresh cilantro

2 teaspoons freshly squeezed lemon juice

24 store-bought wonton wrappers

Cornstarch slurry (see page 26)

3 cups canola oil

MAKE IT EASIER: *Leftover mashed potatoes make this filling richer and creamier!*

1. **Make the filling:** In a large saucepan, combine the potatoes, 1 tablespoon of salt, and enough water to cover. Bring to a boil. Reduce the heat and simmer the potatoes for 10 to 12 minutes, or until soft. Reserve 1 cup of cooking water and drain the potatoes. Set the potatoes aside to dry for 5 minutes.

2. Place the saucepan over medium-high heat and add the butter to melt. Add the shallot, garlic, and ginger and sauté for about 30 seconds until fragrant. Stir in the curry powder and cook for 20 seconds more, stirring. Add the potatoes and toss to coat with the curry butter.

3. Turn off the heat and mash the potatoes until well combined. Season with 1 teaspoon of salt. The mixture should be lumpy but thoroughly combined. Fold in the peas, cilantro, and lemon juice. Set aside to cool.

4. **Fold the dumplings:** While working, keep the wrappers covered.

5. Lay 6 wrappers on a cutting board and place 1 tablespoon of filling in the center of each. Moisten the edges of the wrapper with cornstarch slurry.

6. Fold the dumplings using the Parcel Fold (see page 29). Repeat with the remaining wrappers and filling.

7. **Cook and serve:** In a wok or Dutch oven over medium-high heat, heat the canola oil to 375°F. Set a wire rack over a sheet pan and set aside.

VEGETARIAN

8. Working in batches of 4 to 6 dumplings, gently lower the dumplings into the hot oil. Use a skimmer to flip the dumplings or to keep them submerged in the hot oil. Fry for 4 to 5 minutes, or until browned and crispy.

9. Using a skimmer, transfer the dumplings from the hot oil to the prepared rack. Sprinkle with the remaining 2 teaspoons of salt and serve hot.

FIVE-SPICE CHICKEN BAOS

MAKES 24 dumplings **PREP TIME** 35 minutes, plus 30 minutes to proof
COOK TIME 30 minutes

Five-spice powder is a classic blend of star anise, cinnamon, cloves, fennel seeds, and Sichuan peppercorns that makes these baos irresistible. When cooking the cauliflower for these baos, get it nice and charred to develop maximum flavor. You can also use green beans or asparagus, if you prefer.

3 tablespoons vegetable oil, divided

1 cup roughly chopped cauliflower florets

2 garlic cloves, minced

½-inch piece fresh ginger, peeled and grated

2 teaspoons Chinese five-spice powder

Pinch kosher salt

Ground white pepper

2 cups shredded cooked chicken

3 scallions, white and green parts, thinly sliced

2 teaspoons sesame oil

1 batch Bao Dough (page 22)

MIX IT UP: *If you're heading to the Asian market, pick up some roast duck and use that instead of chicken in this bao. It's so tasty!*

1. **Make the filling:** In a large skillet over medium-high heat, add 1 tablespoon of vegetable oil, swirling to coat the skillet. When the oil begins to smoke, add the cauliflower and sear for 2 to 3 minutes, or until the cauliflower begins to char. Add the garlic and ginger and sauté for about 15 seconds until fragrant. Add the five-spice powder and season with salt and white pepper to taste.

2. Remove from the heat and stir in the chicken, scallions, and sesame oil. Transfer to a large bowl and set aside to cool.

3. **Prepare the dough and shape the baos:** Line a sheet pan with parchment paper and set aside.

4. Cut the dough into 24 equal pieces (see page 24). Keep the dough pieces covered under plastic wrap.

5. Use your fingertips to flatten and stretch one piece of dough into a 4-inch circle. Place the circle flat on one palm. Spoon 1 heaping tablespoon of filling into the center. Gather the edges of the dough together and pinch tightly at the top. Place the bao, pinched-side up, on the prepared sheet pan, leaving about 2 inches between each bao. Repeat with the remaining dough and filling.

6. Loosely cover the buns and let rise for 20 to 30 minutes, or until they feel puffy.

7. **Cook and serve:** In a large nonstick skillet over medium-high heat, heat 1 tablespoon of vegetable oil until shimmering. Arrange half the buns in the skillet, leaving ½ inch of space between each bun. Pan-fry for 30 seconds, or until the bun bottoms are golden brown.

8. Pour ¼ cup water into the skillet and cover the pan. Cook for 8 to 10 minutes, or until the water evaporates completely. Turn off the heat and leave the lid on for 1 minute, or until the sizzling stops. The baos should have bottoms that are golden brown and crispy. Transfer to a warm plate and repeat the process with the remaining buns and oil.

Smashed Cucumber Salad, page 94

6

SOUPS, SIDE SNACKS, AND DIPPING SAUCES

Dumplings are infinitely better when paired with a flavorful dipping sauce. You can make a meal from a variety of dumplings by adding a soup, side dish, or plate of noodles. This chapter features an assortment of soups to which you can add any number of dumplings for a comforting bowl of dumpling soup. You'll also find classic condiments such as Chili Crisp Sauce (page 99) and its savory cousin, XO Sauce (page 100).

WONTON SOUP BROTH

SERVES 4 to 6 **PREP TIME** 20 minutes **COOK TIME** 2 hours 15 minutes

A rich, savory broth is essential to an excellent wonton soup. This recipe calls for premade chicken stock for more flavor instead of starting with water. Traditional Soup Wontons (page 37) make a classic combination with this broth, but you can also serve it with Fish and Napa Cabbage Dumplings (page 40).

2 pounds chicken parts (backs, necks, feet, wings)

8 ounces ham hocks or salt pork

4 cups chicken stock

½ head Napa cabbage, cut into chunks

¼ cup dried shrimp

4 scallions, white and green parts separated, thinly sliced

4-inch piece fresh ginger, peeled

1 star anise pod

Kosher salt

Light soy sauce, for seasoning

1 batch cooked Traditional Soup Wontons (page 37)

2 tablespoons sesame oil

COOKING TIP: *To save time and make a richer broth, use a pressure cooker for step 2 for 40 minutes.*

1. In a large stockpot, combine the chicken and ham hocks and cover with water. Bring to a boil and cook for 10 minutes. Drain the contents and rinse with cold water to remove any coagulated blood and foam. Return to the stockpot.

2. Add the chicken broth and enough water to cover the bones by at least 1 inch. Add the cabbage, dried shrimp, scallion whites, ginger, and star anise. Bring to a boil over high heat, then reduce the heat to low and simmer, uncovered, for about 2 hours. Using tongs or a skimmer, remove and discard the solid pieces from the broth.

3. Line a fine-mesh strainer with cheesecloth, set it over a large saucepan, and strain the broth. Season to taste with salt and soy sauce.

4. Divide the cooked wontons and soup among 4 to 6 warmed bowls. Garnish with sesame oil and the scallion greens to serve.

SHIITAKE MUSHROOM WONTON SOUP BROTH

SERVES 4 to 6 **PREP TIME** 10 minutes **COOK TIME** 40 minutes

This vegan version of the classic wonton soup with Tofu and Carrot Wontons (page 43) calls for premade vegetable stock as the base, which is fortified with mushrooms and aromatics. If you can't find mushroom soy sauce, just add more dried mushrooms to the soup.

4 cups vegetable stock

½ head Napa cabbage, cut into chunks

4 dried shiitake mushrooms

4-inch piece fresh ginger, slightly smashed

2 garlic cloves, slightly smashed

4 scallions, white and green parts separated, thickly sliced

Kosher salt

Mushroom soy sauce, for seasoning

1 batch cooked Tofu and Carrot Wontons (page 43)

2 tablespoons sesame oil

MIX IT UP: *You don't have to stick to vegetarian wontons. Use this broth for pork wontons or wontons with any of the dumpling fillings in this book, if having a vegan dish is not a concern for you.*

1. In a medium stockpot, combine the vegetable stock, cabbage, mushrooms, ginger, garlic, and scallion whites. Bring to a boil over high heat, then reduce the heat to medium-low and simmer for 20 minutes, or until the mushrooms are rehydrated.

2. Using a slotted spoon, remove the mushrooms from the stock. Trim off the mushroom stems and thinly slice the caps. Set aside.

3. Line a fine-mesh strainer with cheesecloth, set it over a large saucepan, and strain the broth, discarding the solids. Return the sliced mushrooms to the stock and simmer over low heat for 10 minutes. Season to taste with salt and mushroom soy sauce.

4. Divide the cooked wontons and soup among 4 to 6 warmed bowls. Garnish with sesame oil and the scallion greens to serve.

VEGAN

COCONUT CURRY SOUP

SERVES 4 to 6 **PREP TIME** 10 minutes **COOK TIME** 35 minutes

As the winter months drag on, the dry, cold air makes me crave richer soups like this sooth-ing coconut curry soup served with Spicy Shrimp Dumplings (page 47). I like to think the coconut milk is nourishing my skin from the inside out.

2 tablespoons coconut oil or vegetable oil

1 medium onion, chopped

1-inch piece fresh ginger, peeled and minced

4 garlic cloves, minced

1 tablespoon yellow curry powder

2 cups vegetable stock

Generous pinch kosher salt

2 (14-ounce) cans coconut milk

1 batch cooked Spicy Shrimp Dumplings (page 47)

Juice of ½ lime

2 tablespoons roughly chopped fresh cilantro

COOKING TIP: *Use full-fat coconut milk for the most robust flavor.*

1. In a large saucepan over medium-high heat, heat the coconut oil until it shimmers. Add the onion and sweat for about 7 minutes until soft and translucent. Add the ginger and garlic and sauté for 1 minute, stirring to keep the garlic from browning. Stir in the curry powder and cook for about 30 seconds until fragrant.

2. Add the vegetable stock and bring to a boil. Add the salt and reduce the heat to low. Simmer the broth for 10 minutes, stirring occasionally. Stir in the coconut milk and continue to simmer on low heat for 10 minutes more. Do not let the broth boil.

3. Divide the cooked dumplings and soup among 4 to 6 warmed bowls. Garnish with cilantro to serve.

HOT AND SOUR SOUP

SERVES 4 to 6 **PREP TIME** 10 minutes, plus 20 minutes to soak **COOK TIME** 15 minutes

The spiciness and sourness of this soup balance out the rich Beef and Scallion Dumplings (page 41). Try using thicker dumpling wrappers—the wrappers will soak up the soup and get even tastier!

4 dried shiitake mushrooms

¼ cup unseasoned rice vinegar

2 tablespoons cornstarch

2 tablespoons light soy sauce

2 teaspoons sugar

1 tablespoon Chili Crisp Sauce (page 99) or store-bought chili oil

1 teaspoon ground white pepper

¼-inch piece fresh ginger, peeled and minced

4 cups chicken stock

4 ounces firm tofu, rinsed and cut into ¼-inch strips

1 batch cooked Beef and Scallion Dumplings (page 41)

2 scallions, white and green parts, thinly cut on the diagonal

MAKE IT EASIER: *Make a few batches of dumplings to keep in the freezer, so you can have this delicious soup in a matter of minutes.*

1. Place the mushrooms in a heat-proof bowl and cover them with boiling water. Soak for about 20 minutes until softened. Drain the mushrooms, reserving ¼ cup of soaking liquid in a small bowl. Thinly slice the mushrooms and set aside.

2. Stir the vinegar, cornstarch, soy sauce, sugar, chili crisp sauce, white pepper, and ginger into the reserved mushroom liquid until the cornstarch and sugar dissolve. Set aside.

3. In a large saucepan, bring the chicken stock to a boil. Reduce the heat to medium to keep a simmer and stir in the sliced mushrooms. Simmer for about 2 minutes. Stir in the tofu and simmer for 2 minutes more.

4. Give the cornstarch mixture a quick stir and stir it into the pot. Turn the heat to medium-high and cook the soup for about 30 seconds, stirring, until thickened. Reduce the heat to maintain a simmer.

5. Divide the cooked dumplings and soup among 4 to 6 warmed bowls. Garnish with scallions to serve.

SMASHED CUCUMBER SALAD

SERVES 4 **PREP TIME** 10 minutes

Just one whiff of this cucumber salad mixed with sesame oil and cilantro gets my mouth watering, and I'm instantly hungry. It's a great summer salad when you want something crunchy and refreshing. It pairs beautifully alongside dumplings like Spicy Shrimp Dumplings (page 47) and Xiao Long Bao (page 52).

2 English cucumbers

2 tablespoons rice vinegar

1 tablespoon sesame oil

3 teaspoons sesame seeds, toasted, divided

3 garlic cloves, minced

2 teaspoons light soy sauce

1 teaspoon Chili Crisp Sauce (page 99)

1 teaspoon sugar

½ cup roughly chopped fresh cilantro

COOKING TIP: *This salad is best served immediately, but you can let it marinate for up to 30 minutes before serving.*

1. Lay one cucumber on a clean cutting board. Place the flat side of a cleaver or kitchen knife on the cucumber and pound your fist down the length of the knife, until the cucumber is flattened and split. Repeat with the second cucumber. Cut the cucumbers crosswise into 1-inch chunks and transfer to a medium bowl.

2. In a small bowl, whisk the vinegar, sesame oil, 2 teaspoons of sesame seeds, garlic, soy sauce, chili crisp sauce, and sugar to blend. Pour the mixture over the cucumbers, add the cilantro, and toss to coat. Garnish with the remaining 1 teaspoon of sesame seeds to serve.

VEGAN

PICKLED RADISHES

SERVES 6 to 8 **PREP TIME** 15 minutes, plus overnight to pickle

When I was a kid, my granny came to stay with us for a visit. She liked pickled foods, so my mom made a huge jar of these pickled radishes. Granny ate them with everything, at every meal, and dipped into them as snacks throughout the day. This recipe works well with daikon radish and even carrot sticks.

12 to 15 red radishes, trimmed and quartered

3 fresh ginger slices, each about the size of a quarter, peeled

2 garlic cloves, smashed

1 dried red chile

1 cup rice vinegar

½ cup sugar

1 tablespoon kosher salt

MAKE IT EASIER: *If you want the pickled radishes sooner, thinly slice the radishes instead of quartering them and they should be ready by the time the pickling liquid is cool.*

1. In a clean 24-ounce glass jar, combine the radishes, ginger, garlic, and red chile.

2. In a small saucepan over high heat, combine the vinegar, sugar, ¼ cup water, and the salt. Stir to dissolve the sugar and salt and bring to a boil. Remove from the heat and pour the pickling liquid into the jar to cover the radishes. Set aside for about 1 hour to cool to room temperature. Seal the jar and refrigerate overnight.

3. The pickles will be ready to eat the next day but will improve in flavor within 3 days. They will keep for up to 1 month in the refrigerator.

GLUTEN-FREE

VEGAN

FRIED PEANUTS

SERVES 4 to 6 **PREP TIME** 5 minutes **COOK TIME** 6 minutes

Our favorite Chinese restaurant serves a generous bowl of fried peanuts as a free appetizer as we browse the menu. If you've only ever had roasted peanuts from the grocery store, try this recipe—freshly fried peanuts are a revelation!

3 cups fresh peanuts with skin, rinsed and drained

1 cup vegetable oil or peanut oil

Generous pinch kosher salt

MIX IT UP: *Toss in a pinch of five-spice powder with the salt to boost the flavor.*

1. Line a large plate with paper towels and set aside.

2. In a medium skillet over medium-low heat, combine the peanuts and oil. Cook the peanuts for 5 to 6 minutes, stirring occasionally, or until the nuts smell toasty and you hear a faint popping noise. Gently shake the pan to redistribute the peanuts in the oil so they fry evenly.

3. Using a skimmer, lift the peanuts from the hot oil and transfer to the prepared plate. Set aside to cool slightly. Transfer the slightly cooled peanuts to a large bowl and toss with the salt. Serve warm.

VEGAN ● GLUTEN-FREE

COLD SESAME NOODLE SALAD

SERVES 4 to 6 **PREP TIME** 15 minutes, plus 30 minutes to chill **COOK TIME** 10 minutes

This is a delicious and quick-to-prepare pantry dish. It's a hit at parties and picnics. I like using chunky peanut butter for more texture, but use what you have. Although these noodles are best served cold, I will understand completely if you can't wait that long and just eat them hot.

1 pound dried egg noodles

2 teaspoons sesame oil

½ cup peanut butter

2 tablespoons Chinese sesame paste

2 tablespoons light soy sauce

2 teaspoons rice vinegar

Pinch ground Sichuan pepper

1 small cucumber, peeled and cut into thin strips

3 scallions, white and green parts, thinly sliced

2 tablespoons roughly chopped fresh cilantro

1 tablespoon sesame seeds, toasted

COOKING TIP: *If you can't find Chinese sesame paste, stir together 1½ tablespoons tahini with 2 teaspoons sesame oil instead.*

1. Bring a large pot of water to a boil and cook the noodles according to the package instructions. Reserve ¼ cup of cooking water and drain the noodles. Rinse the noodles under cold water and drain completely. Transfer to a bowl and toss with sesame oil to keep them from sticking. Chill in the refrigerator for 30 minutes, or until cold.

2. Meanwhile, in a large bowl, whisk the reserved cooking water, peanut butter, sesame paste, soy sauce, vinegar, and Sichuan pepper until smooth. Set aside.

3. Toss the chilled noodles in the peanut sauce until evenly coated. Transfer the noodles to a serving platter. Garnish with cucumber, scallions, cilantro, and sesame seeds. Serve immediately.

4. Refrigerate leftovers, covered, for up to 5 days.

VEGETARIAN

SOY-VINEGAR DIPPING SAUCE

MAKES ½ cup **PREP TIME** 5 minutes **COOK TIME** 5 minutes

Here is a classic dipping sauce to serve with dumplings. The acidity in the vinegar helps cut through the richness of the dumplings. When having people over, make a triple batch and provide everyone with a small dish of their own so they can double dip all they want.

¼ cup soy sauce

3 tablespoons black vinegar

2 teaspoons sugar

1 teaspoon paper-thin sliced scallion, green part only

COOKING TIP: *Black vinegar is like Chinese balsamic vinegar. If you can't find black vinegar, substitute 2½ tablespoons balsamic vinegar plus 2 teaspoons rice vinegar.*

VEGAN

In a small saucepan over low heat, combine the soy sauce, vinegar, 2 tablespoons water, and the sugar. Heat for 5 minutes, or until the sugar is dissolved. Remove from the heat and transfer to a small bowl. Sprinkle in the scallion.

CHILI CRISP SAUCE

MAKES about 1 cup **PREP TIME** 5 minutes **COOK TIME** 2 minutes, plus 20 minutes to cool

This sauce is all about minimal effort for maximum payoff. Its fiery red color and flavor can perk up any dish, especially dumplings! But you can add this to everything from scrambled eggs to steamed rice, and even avocado toast!

4 tablespoons Sichuan chili flakes

2 tablespoons white sesame seeds

1 star anise pod

1 cinnamon stick

1 teaspoon kosher salt

1 cup vegetable oil

COOKING TIP: *To achieve the bright red color, you need Sichuan chili flakes. For a spicier sauce, add a few more tablespoons of chili flakes or try gochugaru, or Korean chili flakes.*

1. In a medium heat-proof bowl, stir together the chili flakes, sesame seeds, star anise, cinnamon stick, and salt and set aside.

2. In a wok or skillet over medium-high heat, heat the oil. When it just begins to smoke, turn off the heat and carefully pour the hot oil over the spices. The mixture will sizzle and bubble up. Let cool for about 20 minutes, or until cooled completely.

3. Stir the sauce. Remove and discard the cinnamon stick and star anise. Transfer the sauce to an air-tight jar. Refrigerate until ready to use, and up to 3 to 4 weeks.

GLUTEN-FREE

VEGAN

XO SAUCE

MAKES 2½ cups **PREP TIME** 15 minutes **COOK TIME** 15 minutes

XO sauce is a spicy seafood-based condiment from Hong Kong, China that packs a savory punch. Dried scallops can be a bit pricey, but necessary, for this sauce. You can find them at most Asian markets or online. Keep this sauce in the fridge in an airtight container for up to 1 month.

3 ounces large dried scallops

20 dried red chiles, stemmed

2 fresh red chiles, chopped

2 shallots, chopped

2 garlic cloves, chopped

3 ounces small dried shrimp

2 ounces bacon, minced

⅓ cup vegetable oil

1 tablespoon dark brown sugar

2 teaspoons Chinese five-spice powder

2 tablespoons Shaoxing rice wine

COOKING TIP: *When cooking this sauce, open a window and turn on your exhaust fan—the chiles can be overpowering.*

1. Place the scallops in a large glass bowl and cover with boiling water by 1 inch. Soak for 10 minutes, or until the scallops are soft. Reserve 2 tablespoons of soaking water, then drain the remaining liquid. Cover the bowl and microwave the scallops on high power for 3 minutes. Set aside.

2. Once cooled, use your fingers to rub the scallops together to loosen into thin shreds about ¼ inch long. Transfer to a clean bowl and set aside.

3. In a food processor, combine the dried chiles, fresh chiles, shallots, and garlic. Pulse until minced, scraping down the sides of the bowl occasionally. Add the mixture to the scallops.

4. In the food processor (no need to clean it), combine the shrimp and bacon. Pulse until minced.

5. Heat a skillet or wok over medium-high heat. Add the vegetable oil and swirl to coat the skillet. Add the shrimp and bacon and cook for 1 to 2 minutes until the bacon is browned and crispy. Sprinkle in the brown sugar and five-spice powder and cook for about 1 minute until the sugar caramelizes.

6. Reduce the heat to medium and add the scallop and chili-garlic mixture. Cook for 1 to 2 minutes, or until the garlic begins to caramelize. Add the rice wine and cook for 2 to 3 minutes until the wine evaporates. Transfer the sauce to a bowl and let cool.

SWEET CHILI DIPPING SAUCE

MAKES about 2 cups **PREP TIME** 10 minutes **COOK TIME** 20 minutes

Thai sweet chili sauce is available in most Asian markets, but it's easy to make at home, which allows you to control the amount of sweetness and heat. The finished sauce should have a perfect balance of sweet, hot, and savory. Serve with Crab Rangoons (page 78) or Turkey and Napa Cabbage Potstickers (page 82).

½ cup rice vinegar

½ cup sugar

2 tablespoons fish sauce

2 tablespoons Shaoxing rice wine

3 garlic cloves, minced

1 tablespoon red pepper flakes

1½ tablespoons cornstarch

MIX IT UP: *For a fresher, less spicy flavor, use 2 or 3 fresh Thai bird chiles, minced, if you can find them.*

1. In a saucepan over medium-high heat, combine the vinegar, sugar, 3 tablespoons of cold water, the fish sauce, rice wine, garlic, and red pepper flakes. Bring to a boil. Reduce the heat to medium-low and simmer for 10 minutes, stirring occasionally, or until the sauce is reduced by half.

2. In a small bowl, stir together ¼ cup water and the cornstarch until dissolved. Add the the cornstarch slurry to the sauce and cook for about 2 minutes, stirring, until the sauce thickens. Remove from the heat and transfer to a bowl to cool before using.

3. Refrigerate, covered, for up to 3 days.

GLUTEN-FREE

SCALLION-GINGER OIL

MAKES about 2 cups **PREP TIME** 5 minutes **COOK TIME** 25 minutes

This robust oil is my secret ingredient for adding extra flavor to virtually any dish—just a dab gives an amazing flavor pop! You can use the oil hot or cold. Keep a small jar in your refrigerator, so it's always on hand. Serve with Shui Jiao (page 36) or Fish and Napa Cabbage Dumplings (page 40).

4 to 6 scallions, white and green parts, thinly sliced

2-inch piece fresh ginger, peeled and grated or finely chopped

1 teaspoon kosher salt

1 cup vegetable oil

COOKING TIP: *This oil is a great way to use up bits of scallion and ginger hanging around in your fridge. Don't let them go to waste.*

1. In a medium heat-proof bowl, stir together the scallions, ginger, and salt to combine. Set aside.

2. In a wok or skillet over medium-high heat, heat the vegetable oil until it just begins to smoke. Remove the wok from the heat and, carefully and slowly, pour the hot oil over the scallions and ginger, so it does not bubble over. Let the mixture cool for about 20 minutes, or until cooled completely.

3. Refrigerate in an airtight jar until ready to use, or up to 3 days.

GLUTEN-FREE

VEGAN

Measurements and Conversions

US STANDARD	US STANDARD (ounces)	METRIC (approximate)
2 tablespoons	1 fl. oz.	30 mL
¼ cup	2 fl. oz.	60 mL
½ cup	4 fl. oz.	120 mL
1 cup	8 fl. oz.	240 mL
1½ cups	12 fl. oz.	355 mL
2 cups or 1 pint	16 fl. oz.	475 mL
4 cups or 1 quart	32 fl. oz.	1 L
1 gallon	128 fl. oz.	4 L
⅛ teaspoon	————	0.5 mL
¼ teaspoon	————	1 mL
½ teaspoon	————	2 mL
¾ teaspoon	————	4 mL
1 teaspoon	————	5 mL
1 tablespoon	————	15 mL
¼ cup	————	59 mL
⅓ cup	————	79 mL
½ cup	————	118 mL
⅔ cup	————	156 mL
¾ cup	————	177 mL
1 cup	————	235 mL
2 cups or 1 pint	————	475 mL
3 cups	————	700 mL
4 cups or 1 quart	————	1 L
½ gallon	————	2 L
1 gallon	————	4 L
½ ounce	————	15 g
1 ounce	————	30 g
2 ounces	————	60 g
4 ounces	————	115 g
8 ounces	————	225 g
12 ounces	————	340 g
16 ounces or 1 pound	————	455 g

FAHRENHEIT (F)	CELSIUS (C) (approximate)
250°F	120°C
300°F	150°C
325°F	180°C
375°F	190°C
400°F	200°C
425°F	220°C
450°F	230°C

Resources

99 Ranch Market (99Ranch.com): There are 51 stores across seven states specializing in Chinese groceries and products. Here, you can buy proteins, seafood, dry goods, spices, condiments, fresh noodles, and produce. They even have an online shop where you can order items to be shipped to you if there isn't a store near you.

Amazon (Amazon.com): You can buy virtually any piece of equipment or pantry ingredient needed for dumplings on Amazon.

H Mart (Hmart.com): With 71 locations nationwide, this Korean American supermarket chain carries pan-Asian produce and imported goods, including Korean and Chinese staples.

Sur La Table (SurLaTable.com): I mentioned that my favorite nonstick skillets and woks are the ceramic titanium nonstick pans made by Scanpan. Made in Denmark from 100 percent recycled aluminum, these are investment pieces and indispensable for all kinds of cooking, not just for making dumplings. Sur La Table has been selling top quality kitchenware since 1972 and is the largest seller of Scanpan products in the United States.

The Wok Shop (WokShop.com/newstore): A local favorite in San Francisco's Chinatown, it is a shop jam-crammed full of woks, steamer baskets, spiders, and everything else you need for making dumplings. Visit in person, if you can, or online.

Index

Acknowledgments

Gratitude goes to the entire team at Callisto Media, especially my editor, Annie Choi, whose patient encouragement guided me to complete this book. Thanks to Ada Fung who developed this concept with clarity and insight. Thank you both for trusting me with your vision.

Special thanks to Cynthia Shum, who went along with Devyn's wish to celebrate his birthday with an unforgettable dumpling-making party. The memories of that wonderful class carried me through writing this book.

Most importantly, thanks to Mr. B for his support and jumping in to make dinner while I wrote this book! I love you so much!

About the Author

 **CHEF TERRI DIEN** is a native New Yorker living in the San Francisco Bay Area. She left political consulting in 2003 to pursue her lifelong passion and enrolled in City College of San Francisco's Culinary Arts and Hospitality Studies program. Dien has worked in restaurants, in both savory and pastry roles, and enjoyed a 15-year teaching career for Draeger's Cooking School, South San Francisco Parks and Recreation, and Sur La Table. Currently, she is executive chef for the Child Care Program at Google. Terri Dien lives in San Mateo, California, with her husband, Paul, and their two cats, Sarah and Henry. Keep in touch with @ChefTerriDien on Instagram!